Fun, Fast
FUSIES

FRIEDA L. ANDERSON

Love to
Quilt...

Located in Paducah, Kentucky, the American Quilter's Society (AQS) is dedicated to promoting the accomplishments of today's quilters. Through its publications and events, AQS strives to honor today's quiltmakers and their work and to inspire future creativity and innovation in quiltmaking.

EDITOR: TONI TOOMEY
COPY EDITOR: CHRYSTAL ABHALTER
GRAPHIC DESIGN: AMY CHASE
COVER DESIGN: MICHAEL BUCKINGHAM
QUILT PHOTOS: CHARLES R. LYNCH
HOW-TO-PHOTOGRAPHY: FRIEDA ANDERSON

Library of Congress Cataloging-in-Publication Data

Anderson, Frieda L.
    Fun, fast fusies: love to quilt / by Frieda L. Anderson.
        p. cm.
    Summary: "Fused appliqué technique explained and full-sized patterns provided for hand and machine sewing"--Provided by publisher.
    ISBN 1-57432-888-3
    1. Appliqué--Patterns. 2. Patchwork--Patterns. 3. Quilting--Patterns.
I. Title.

TT779.A575 2005
746.44'5041--dc22

                        2005010273

Additional copies of this book may be ordered from the American Quilter's Society, PO Box 3290, Paducah, KY 42002-3290, or call 1-800-626-5420 or online at www.AmericanQuilter.com.

Dedication

To my fellow deans at the Chicago School of Fusing for all your help and support.

Acknowledgments

I am eternally grateful to my beloved husband who always allowed me to play with my fabric, even if he made me keep it organized, and to my wonderful boys—Lars, Erik, and Zachary—who acknowledge me as an artist. I could never have been this successful without the love and support of my mother, sister, and dear friends who have always supported me in all that I have pursued. And, of course, to my editor who pulled this all together into a cohesive book.

Table of Contents

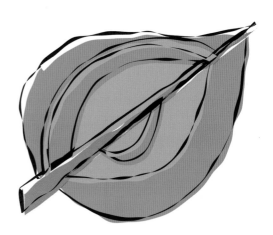

This book is full of fused and quilted artwork. Why fuse? I fuse my fabric art because fusing is fun, fast, and easy. It allows me to use fabric in any shape I want. Instead of worrying about matching up seams of irregular shapes, I can layer irregular shapes and simply fuse them together. This allows me to "draw" any picture my imagination can possibly think of. Fusing offers me both speed and great artistic freedom.

The quilts in this book are my original designs that I am sharing with you. Many of them are smaller versions of larger quilts I have made. All are reflections of my daily life. Many come from photos I have taken of my garden or from my daily walks in the woods with my dog George. I encourage you to make your own designs that reflect your life, either from pictures that you have taken or from drawings of things you like. This way you will be making your own art from the world around you.

I am showing you how I make my art quilts and hope that after you have tried a few projects in this book you will begin to explore your own art quilts. By fusing them you can make many, many small art quilts and explore your own creative desires.

To begin with, use 100 percent cotton fabric. Hand-dyed cottons work best. Use fabrics that are tightly woven. It is difficult to get fusible web to adhere to fabrics with permanent press or other finishes on the fabric.

Wash and iron your fabrics before fusing. Press all of your fabrics and batting with steam so that no wrinkles remain before applying fusible web to the fabric.

Follow the manufacturer's directions that come on your fusible web.

The projects in this book call for pressing the fused fabrics more than once or twice. Use only as much heat as necessary in each step. Overheating the fusible web can make it less effective for the final steps in fusing.

If you like, you can fuse all your fabrics at once. This will allow you to work on your design and not have to start and stop all the time to go back and fuse more fabric. Leave the release paper attached to the fused fabric until you are ready to use it.

Take care of the release paper after peeling it off the fabric. You will be using the release paper over and over again for tracing and transferring design pieces to your fabric, and for protecting your iron and work surface from stray bits of fusible web.

Let your fabric cool before removing the release paper. Avoid tearing the release paper as you remove it. Starting at a corner, bend the release paper back and forth until you can lift up an edge and then use your whole hand as a wedge between the fabric and the release paper as you peel it away.

Bubbles can be eliminated after you peel off the release paper. Also, areas can be re-fused without ruining the effectiveness of the fusible.

It's easier to keep fusible web off your iron and work surface than it is to remove it. Keep iron cleaner handy in case of mishaps. Used fabric-softener sheets are good for cleaning your iron. I keep a supply next to my ironing board.

Quick Fused Binding

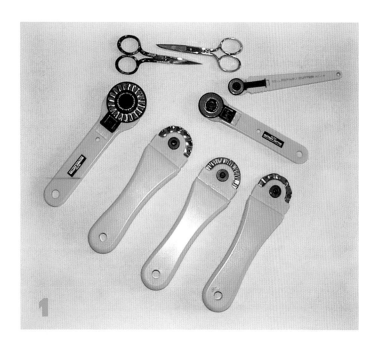

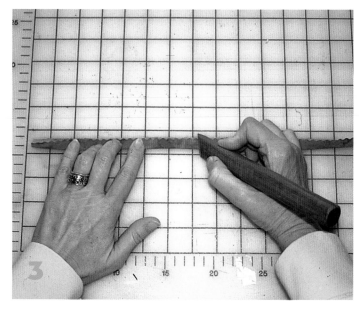

Decorative rotary blades like the ones shown in figure 1 are the secret behind making fun, quick fused bindings.

Cutting Your Binding Strips

1. Wash your binding fabric and steam press it to remove any wrinkles or creasaes.

2. Apply fusible web to the wrong side of your fabrics (See Tips on Fusing on page 5.) Allow the fabric to cool, then peel off the relaease paper. Set the release paper aside for the moment.

3. With a plain rotary blade, cut four strips between 1¼" and 2" wide, depending on how wide you prefer your binding. (Remember, your finished binding will be ½ the width of your strips.) Cut two of the strips the width of your quilt, and cut two strips the length of your quilt plus 2" (fig. 2).

4. Trim one side of each strip with a decorative blade.

5. Fold the binding in half along the long edge, and press it with your fingernail or with a creasing tool. *Do not use* an iron at this point (fig. 3).

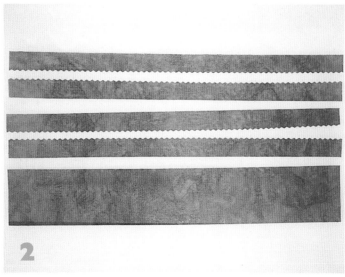

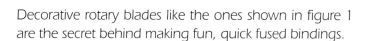

6. Start with one of the short binding strips. Position it against one edge of the quilt, butting it into the crease, and fuse it in place. Turn the quilt over and fuse again (fig 4).

4

7. Repeat step 6 on the opposite edges of the quilt.

8. With the remaining two sides, position the binding and fuse *lightly* in place.

9. On the back of the quilt, peel up the back edge at the end and fold ½" of the front around to the back, folding it over the edge of the quilt. Place a piece of fusible web under the turned over edge and press the rest of the binding down (fig. 5).

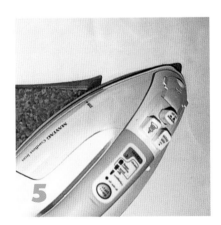

5

10. Use decorative threads to topstitch in place on the front if so desired. You can use the fancy stitches on your machine to create additional patterns with the topstitching.

Signing Your Work

I always put a label on the back of any quilt that I make. My mother drilled into me to always write names and dates on the backs of photos. This has carried over to my quilting. I make my labels on the computer.

1. Create the labels in a word-processing program, such as Microsoft Word.

2. Apply fusible web to a light-colored fabric 9" x 11½". Leave the release paper attached and trim the fabric to 8½" x 11".

3. Put this fabric through your printer to print the label.

4. Now you can cut your label with a decorative blade rotary cutter and fuse it to the back of your quilt.

Beet

BEET, 15" x 20". Made by the author.

This quilt will allow you to get your feet wet with all the techniques. It is a simple and fun quilt to make for your kitchen or for a friend. This is a less complex design than some of the others in this book, which means you will have a free hand with laying out the design.

Material	Amount
dark green for background fabric	½ yd
four greens in various shades for leaves (B, C, D, and E pieces)...a scrap each or 1 fat eighth each	
yellow-green for frame (piece A)	¼ yd or 1 fat quarter
pink, red, and fuchsia for beet (pieces F, G, and H)	a scrap of each or 1 fat eighth of each
lavender, yellow, and blue for the small circles	a scrap of each
fusible web	2 yd
batting	½ yd
backing	½ yd
binding	½ yd

you will also need: extra-fine-tip permanent marker
plain white copy paper 4–10 sheets
very sharp small scissors • rotary mat • rotary cutter
decorative wavy blade for a regular size rotary cutter (optional)

Preparing Your Background

1. Before you begin, steam press all of your fabrics and your batting to remove any wrinkles or creases. Then turn off the steam and use a hot iron for all of the fusing.

2. Apply fusible web to the wrong side of your background fabric. Let the fabric and fusible web cool, then peel away the release paper (fig. 6). (See Tips on Fusing on page 5.) Set aside the release paper to use later.

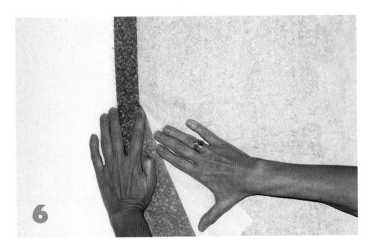
6

3. Place the background fabric on a cutting mat with the fusible side up, and cut a piece 15½" x 20½" (about ½" larger than the finished quilt size).

4. Cut a piece of batting 16" x 21", and place your background fabric fusible side down on top of your batting piece. Fuse the background to the batting, following the manufacturer's directions for the fusible web. Set this aside while you prepare your design pieces.

Making Your Design Pieces

Now we can start the fun stuff—making the design pieces for your quilt. Just in case you are tempted to fuse the design pieces to your background as you go, don't! As you will see later, there will be a specific order in which you fuse the design pieces to the background.

1. Apply fusible web to the wrong sides of the fabrics you plan to use for your design pieces. Let each fabric cool, but for now leave the release paper attached to the fused web.

2. Let's start with the light green leaves (design pieces labeled B). Remove the release paper from the fusible web on the fabric you plan to use for the light green leaves.

3. Find the pieces labeled B in the BEET pattern on pages 12–15. Place release paper from fabric B on top of the pattern and use the extra-fine-tip permanent marker to trace the design pieces labeled B. Leave yourself plenty of space between the design pieces. Place the release paper ink side down on the fusible side of fabric B.

4. Place an extra piece of release paper over the traced release paper and fabric to protect your iron from any exposed fusible web (you can use the piece of release paper from your background fabric). Press lightly with a hot iron to transfer the permanent ink to the back side of the fused fabric. Don't press long—just long enough to transfer the marker to the fused fabric (fig. 7).

7

If you are unsure how long to press, practice first on a test piece. You can always lift up a corner of the release paper, not peeling it all off, to see if the marker has transferred to the fabric (fig. 7, page 9). You do not want to overheat at this point as the fusible can get fused up!

5. Allow the fabric to cool and then peel away the release paper. (By removing the paper before cutting you get a very clean, crisp cut edge.) Cut the design pieces, using very sharp small scissor (fig. 8). On very light colored fabrics, be sure to cut away all of the marker lines. Set your light green leaves aside.

6. Repeat steps 2 through 5 for the rest of the labeled design pieces. You can trace the circle pieces from the pattern on pages 12–15, or you can cut the circles freehand. For now, don't cut the frame pieces (yellow-green pieces labeled A) or the circles that you will add to the frame.

Assembling Your BEET Design

1. Let's start with the beet. Layer the beet leaves and the beet pieces, fusible-side down, on top of a piece of release paper. When the beet and its leaves all look right to you,

cover them with another piece of release paper and lightly fuse them together to create one unit (fig. 9). Set your beet aside for now.

2. For the frame sides, remove the release paper from your yellow-green fabric and place the fabric fusible-side up on your rotary mat. Cut two strips about ½" x 12" with your rotary cutter, using a gentle, slightly curving motion. Using the same curving motion, cut two more strips about ½" x 10". This could be a place to use a decorative rotary blade to add an interesting design element to your quilt.

3. Position the frame pieces on the dark green background, using the assembly diagram on page 11 as a guide. You don't have to be exact. Just eyeball the placement of the pieces and adjust their positions according to what looks good to you.

4. Place your beet in the center of the frame you created and arrange the light and medium green leaves around the frame. (You will add the circles later.)

5. Once the design looks right to you, cover it with release paper, and fuse the design in place.

Finishing Your Quilt

1. Layer your quilt top with a piece of backing fabric 17" x 22", and press well. Pin along the outside edges with safety pins to hold the layers in place.

2. Outline the quilt around the frame, the leaves, and the beet. I like to use all my decorative threads at this point and change the color to go with the color of the design piece I'm outlining (fig. 10).

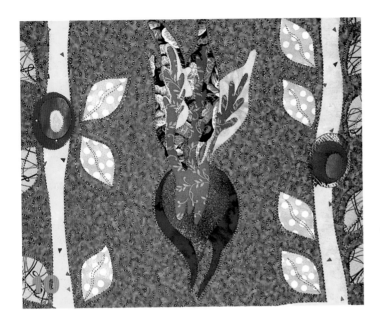

3. Cut your circles freehand or follow the directions for tracing with the marker. Place these on top of the frame either in the way it is shown or to your liking. Outline stitch around these. At this point you can be finished, or you can continue to quilt in the background to your liking.

4. Press the whole quilt top well with a hot iron and steam to make sure all the fused pieces are set. Use a rotary cutter to square up and trim the edges of the quilt, trimming it to

15" x 20". Add a hanging sleeve and a fused or sewn binding of your choice. Be sure to add a label to your quilt.

page 12   page 13

page 14   page 15

BEET quilt assembly

Tomatoes, 10½" x 7½". Made by the author.

Every year in my garden I grow tomatoes and broccoli. These perky little tomatoes will brighten any room you put them in.

Material	Amount
royal blue for background	¼ yd
aqua (piece A)	1 fat eighth
red for tomatoes (pieces R and P)	scraps
dark and light green for leaves (pieces G and L)	scraps
fusible web	1 yd
batting	10" x 13"
backing	1 fat quarter or ½ yd
binding	¼ yd

you will also need: extra-fine-tip permanent marker
very sharp small scissors • rotary mat • rotary cutter

Preparing Your Background

1. Before you begin, steam press all of your fabrics and your batting to remove any wrinkles or creases. Then turn off the steam and use a hot iron for all of the fusing.

2. Apply fusible web to the wrong side of your background fabric. Let the fabric and fusible web cool and peel off the release paper.

3. Place the background fabric on a cutting mat with the fusible side up, and cut a piece 8" x 11" (about ½" larger than the finished quilt size).

4. On the TOMATOES pattern on page 18, find the outline for design piece A. Place the background release paper over the pattern, and use an extra-fine-tip permanent marker to trace ¼" inside the outline design piece A.

5. Place the release paper ink side down on the fusible side of your background fabric. Press lightly with a hot iron to transfer the permanent ink to the back side of the fused fabric. Don't press long—just long enough to transfer the marker to the fused fabric.

5. Allow the fabric to cool and then peel away the release paper. Cut along the transferred line using very sharp small scissors. (In a minute you will cover this hole with the aqua

tomato-background piece.) Position your background fabric back on its release paper right side up.

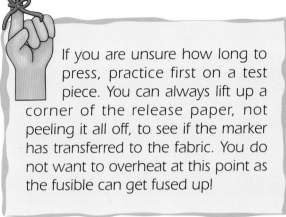

If you are unsure how long to press, practice first on a test piece. You can always lift up a corner of the release paper, not peeling it all off, to see if the marker has transferred to the fabric. You do not want to overheat at this point as the fusible can get fused up!

6. Cut a piece of batting 8½" x 10½", and place your background fusible side down on top of the batting. Fuse the background to the batting, following the manufacturer's directions for the fusible web (fig. 11). Set this aside while you prepare the rest of your design pieces.

7. Remove the release paper from your aqua fabric. Place the release paper over the pattern, and use an extra-fine-tip permanent marker to trace ¼" inside the outline design piece A (fig. 12).

8. Cut design piece A. Cover the hole in the background fabric with this piece and fuse it to the background.

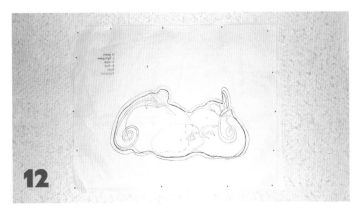

Assembling Your TOMATOES Quilt

1. Let's start with the two large tomatoes (design pieces R and P). Remove the release papers from the fusible web on your tomato fabrics, and trace the tomato design pieces R and P onto the release papers.

2. Press the release papers, ink side down, to the fusible sides of the tomato fabrics to transfer the permanent ink to the fabrics.

3. Cut out the tomatoes and position them, fusible side down, over their aqua background. Layer the tomatoes and fuse them to the aqua background (fig. 13).

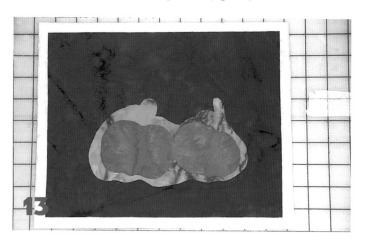

13

4. Position your background and batting on a piece of backing fabric about the same size as the batting, 8" x 11", and press well. Pin along the outside edges with safety pins to hold the layers in place, and outline quilt your tomatoes.

5. Cut out the leaves and curlicues and fuse them to the design. Outline quilt these design pieces with matching thread colors. Then free-motion quilt the royal blue background (fig 14).

14

6. Press the whole quilt top well with a hot iron and steam to make sure all the fused pieces are set. Use a rotary cutter to square up and trim the edges of the quilt, trimming it to 7½" x 10". Add a hanging sleeve and a fused or sewn binding of your choice. Be sure to add a label to your quilt.

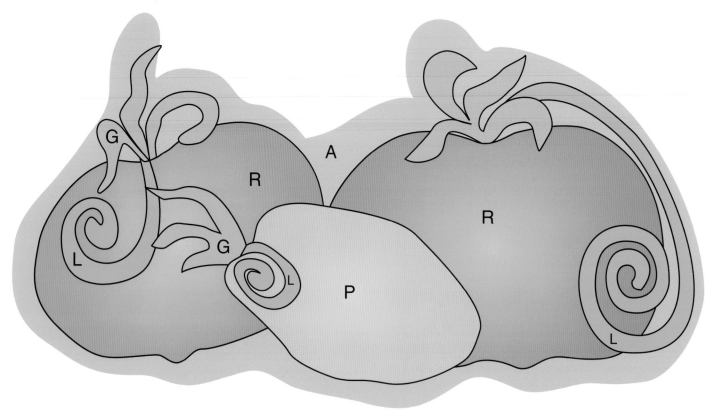

PUMPKIN 15" x 20". Made by the author.

Halloween is one of my favorite holidays. Only Christmas has more decorations at my house than Halloween. I used to grow pumpkins in my garden and this little wall quilt is a direct result of pictures from my pumpkin patch.

Material	Amount
purple/dark pink for background	½ yd
orange for pumpkin (piece O)	1 fat quarter
dark green for leaves (pieces D)	1 fat quarter
light green for leaf veins and curlicues (pieces C)	
medium green for leaf veins (pieces M)	1 fat quarter
brown for stem (piece B)	a scrap or 1 fat eighth
fusible web	2 yd
batting	½ yd
backing	½ yd
binding	½ yd

you will also need: extra-fine-tip permanent marker
plain white copy paper 4–10 sheets
very sharp small scissors • rotary mat • rotary cutter

Preparing Your Background

The instructions for this quilt are very similar to the instructions for making BEET on pages 9–11.

1. Before you begin, steam press all of your fabrics and your batting to remove any wrinkles or creases. Then turn off the steam and use a hot iron for all of the fusing.

2. Apply fusible web to the wrong side of your background fabric. Let the fabric and fusible web cool, then peel away the release paper. Set aside the release paper to use later.

3. Place the background fabric on a cutting mat with the fusible side up, and cut a piece 15½" x 20½" (about ½" larger than the finished quilt size).

4. Cut a piece of batting 17" x 21", and place your background fabric fusible side down on top of your batting piece. Fuse the background to the batting, following the manufacturer's directions for the fusible web.

Making Your Design Pieces

Now we can start the fun stuff—making the design pieces for your quilt. Just in case you are tempted to fuse the design pieces to your background as you go, don't! As you will see later, there will be a specific order in which you fuse the design pieces to the background.

1. Apply fusible web to the wrong sides of the fabrics you plan to use for your design pieces. Let each fabric cool, but for now leave the release paper attached to the fused web.

2. Let's start with the leaves (design pieces labeled D). Remove the release paper from the fusible web on the fabric you plan to use for the leaves.

3. Find design pieces labeled D in the PUMPKIN pattern on pages 22–25. Place the release paper on top of the pattern and use the extra-fine-tip permanent marker to trace the design pieces D.

4. Place the release paper ink side down on the fusible side of your leaf fabric. Press lightly with a hot iron to transfer the permanent ink to the back side of the fused fabric. Don't press long—just long enough to transfer the marker to the fused fabric.

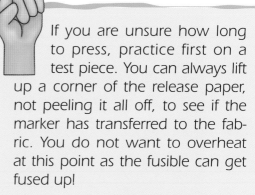

If you are unsure how long to press, practice first on a test piece. You can always lift up a corner of the release paper, not peeling it all off, to see if the marker has transferred to the fabric. You do not want to overheat at this point as the fusible can get fused up!

5. Allow the fabric to cool and then peel away the release paper. (By removing the paper before cutting you get a very clean crisp cut edge.) Cut the design pieces, using very sharp small scissors. On very light colored fabrics, be sure to cut away all of the marker lines. Set your light green leaves aside.

6. Repeat steps 2 through 5 for the rest of the labeled design pieces.

Assembling and Finishing Your PUMPKIN Quilt

1. Study the PUMPKIN quilt assembly diagram on page 21. Notice that the pumpkin overlaps most, but not all, of the leaves and curlicues.

2. Position the leaves on your background, using the quilt assembly diagram as a guide. You don't have to be exact. Just eyeball the placement of the pieces and adjust their positions according to what looks good to you. Then layer the pumpkin, the curlicues, and the remaining leaves

3. Once the whole design looks right to you, remove all but the bottom layer of leaves and fuse these to the background.

4. Layer your quilt top with a piece of backing fabric about the same size as the batting, 17" x 21", and press well. Pin along the outside edges with safety pins to hold the layers in place.

5. Outline quilt this first layer of leaves. I like to use all my decorative threads at this point and change the color to go with the color of the design piece I'm outlining.

6. Fuse the pumpkin to the design, then outline quilt it. Position and fuse the remaining design pieces. Outline quilt these pieces, then free-motion quilt the background (fig. 15).

7. Press the whole quilt top well with a hot iron and steam to make sure all the fused pieces are set. Use a rotary cutter to square up and trim the edges of the quilt, trimming it to 15" x 20". Add a hanging sleeve and a fused or sewn binding of your choice. Be sure to add a label to your quilt.

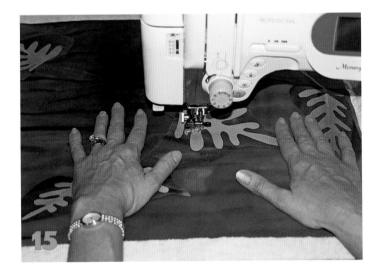

page 22   page 23

page 24   page 25

PUMPKIN quilt assembly

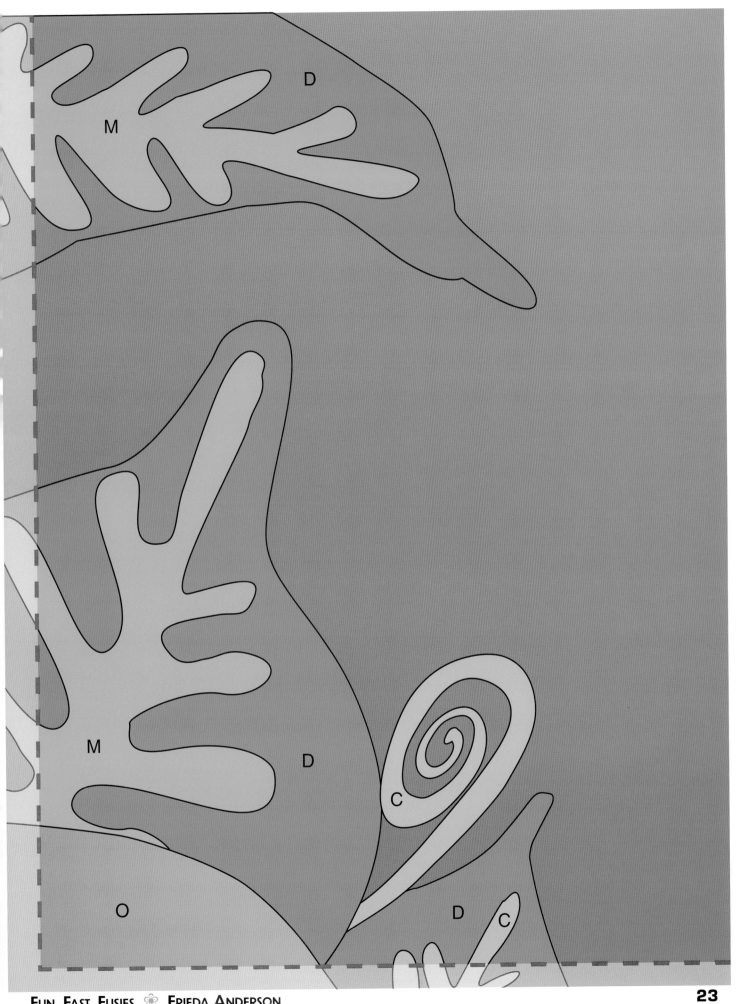

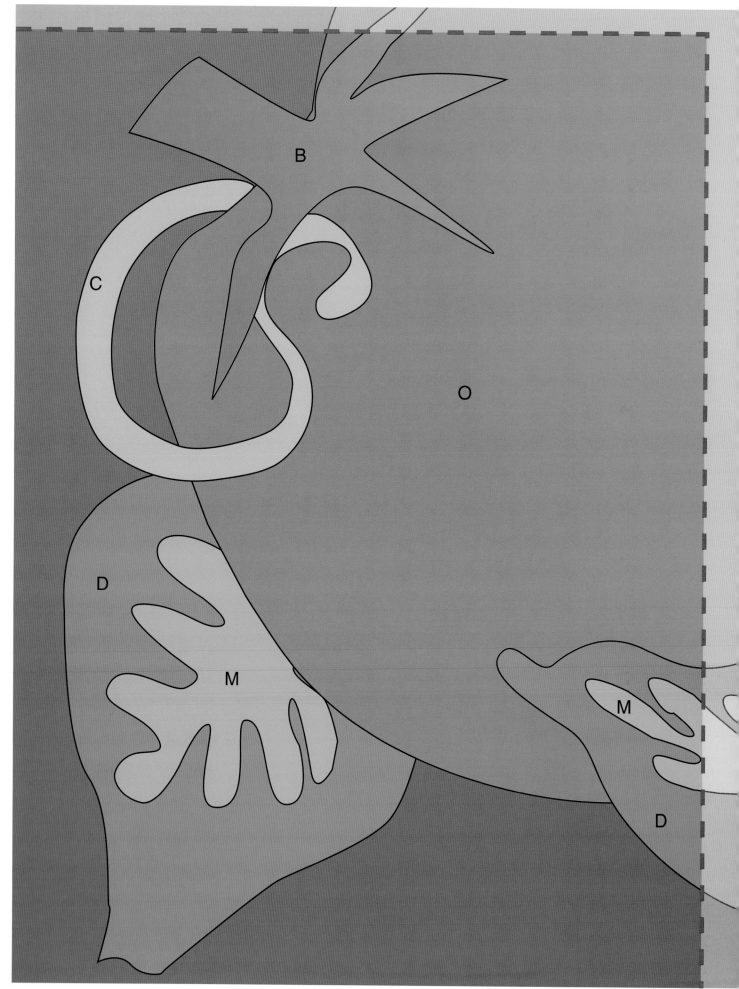

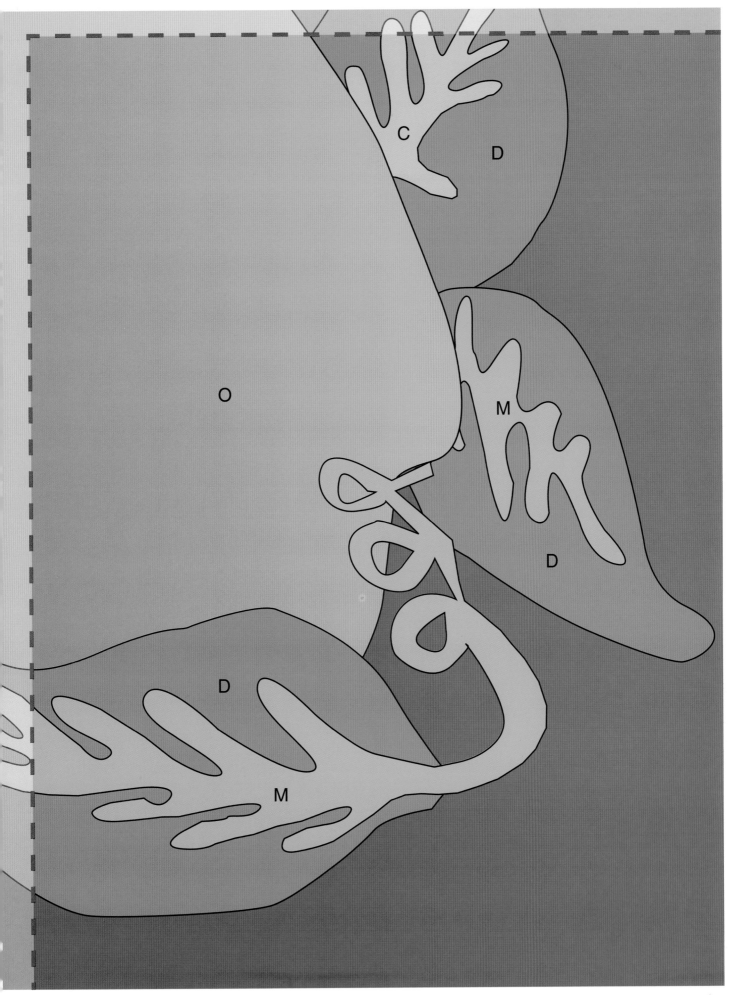

Walk in the Woods, 7½" x 10". Made by the author.

You can draw and cut out the design pieces of this quilt freehand instead of tracing them from the pattern. To give the edges of the leaves a "natural" look, I cut them out with a rotary cutter fitted with a decorative wavy blade.

Material	Amount
red for top band of background	¼ yd or 1 fat quarter
yellow-orange for middle band of background	½ yd or 1 fat quarter
mud green for bottom background band	¼ yd or 1 fat quarter
various greens for leaves (G)	scraps or 1 fat eighth
various aquas and blues for trees (A)	scraps or 1 fat eighth
fusible web	1 yd
batting	8½" x 11" yd
backing	1 fat quarter
binding	1 fat quarter

you will also need: extra-fine-tip permanent marker
very sharp small scissors • rotary mat • rotary cutter
decorative wavy blade for a regular size rotary cutter (optional)

Preparing Your Background

1. Before you begin, steam press all of your fabrics and your batting to remove any wrinkles or creases. Then turn off the steam and use a hot iron for all of the fusing.

2. Apply fusible web to the wrong side of your background fabrics. Let the fabric and fusible web cool, then peel away the release paper. Set aside the release paper to use later.

3. Place the fabrics for the red and mud-green background bands on a cutting mat with the fusible side up, and cut a piece of each fabric 2½" x 10½". Rotary cut a wavy line along one long edge of each fabric.

4. Cut a piece of fabric for the yellow background band 5½" x 10½", and cut a piece of batting 8½" x 11".

5. Center the yellow background band on the batting and fuse it to the batting. Then fuse the red band and the mud-green band above and below the yellow band, using the WALK IN THE WOODS pattern on page 29 as a guide.

6. Layer your background and batting over a backing piece 9" x 11½", and pin the edges to hold the layers together.

7. Stitch in the ditch along the wavy edge of the red band and along the wavy edge of the mud-green band (fig. 16).

16

Assembling Your WALK IN THE WOODS Quilt

1. Let's start with the trees. Remove the release paper from the fusible web on your tree fabric. Use an extra-fine-point permanent marker to trace the trees and branches from the pattern on page 29 onto a piece of release paper. If you like, instead of tracing the leaves, you can draw them freehand onto the release paper.

2. Place release paper ink side down on the fusible side of your tree fabric. Place an extra piece of release paper over the traced release paper and fabric to protect your iron from any exposed fusible web (you can use the piece of release paper from your background fabric). Press lightly with a hot iron to transfer the permanent ink to the back side of the fused fabric. Don't press long—just long enough to transfer the marker to the fused fabric.

3. Allow the fabric to cool and then peel away the release paper. (By removing the paper before cutting you get a very clean crisp cut edge.) Cut out the trees with very sharp small scissors or with a rotary cutter.

4. Lay out your trees onto your background using the WALK IN THE WOODS pattern on page 29 as a guide. Fuse the trees to the background, then outline quilt them (fig. 17, page 28).

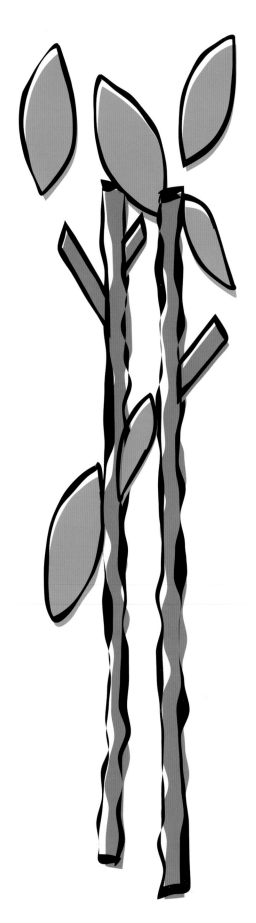

If you are unsure how long to press, practice first on a test piece. You can always lift up a corner of the release paper, not peeling it all off, to see if the marker has transferred to the fabric. You do not want to overheat at this point as the fusible can get fused up!

5. Repeat steps 2 through 4 to make the leaves. Cut out the leaves with a small rotary wavy blade. On very light-colored fabrics, be sure to cut away all of the marker lines.

6. The leaves are not outline quilted. Instead, I hand embroider them to the quilt. You can either outline quilt the leaves or hand embroider them down the center.

7. Press the whole quilt top well with a hot iron and steam to make sure all the fused pieces are set. Use a rotary cutter to square up and trim the edges of the quilt, trimming it to 7½" x 10". Add a hanging sleeve and a fused or sewn binding of your choice. Be sure to add a label to your quilt.

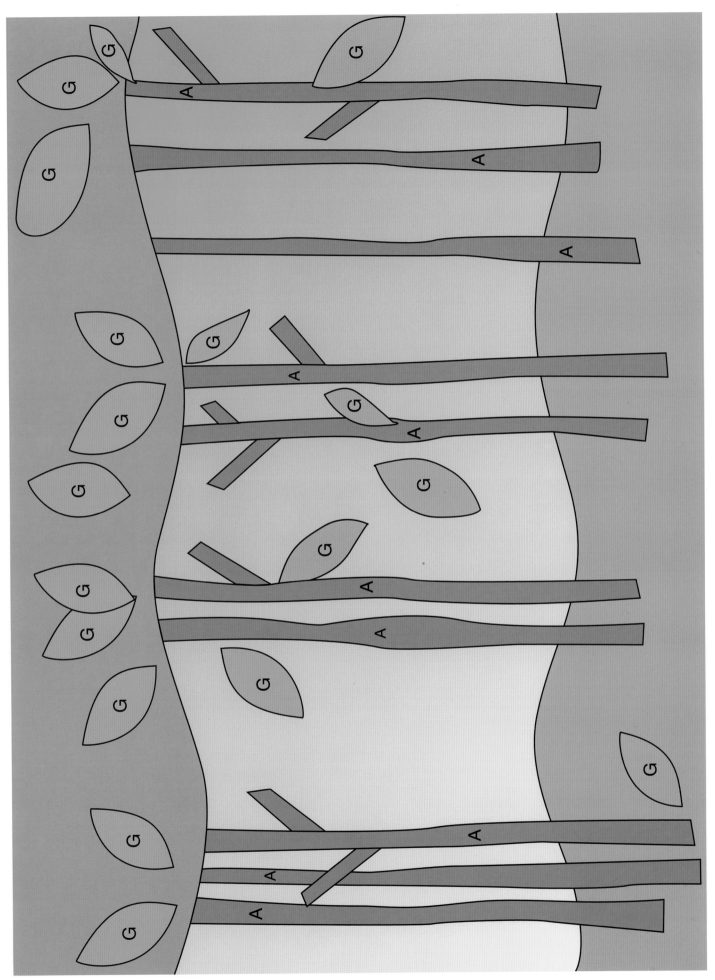

Petite Poppies

PETITE POPPIES, 14" x 16". Made by the author.

I grow poppies in my garden. This quilt is a tribute to the joy they bring me. In the summer, while standing at the kitchen sink doing dishes, I see my poppies out in the garden.

Material	Amount
light lime green for background and flower centers (pieces N)	½ yd
blue-green darker than background, for border	1 yd
light, medium, and medium dark reds and pinks for poppies (pieces L, M, and D)	⅛ yd or 1 fat eighth each
dark purple for poppy centers (pieces U)	a scrap
aqua for stems, leaves, and seed heads, buds, and poppy centers (pieces A and E)	¼ yd or 1 fat quarter (or scraps of different shades of aqua)
fusible web	3 yd
batting	¾ yd
backing	¾ yd
binding	½ yd

you will also need: extra-fine-tip permanent marker
plain white copy paper, 4–10 sheets
very sharp small scissors ▪ rotary mat ▪ rotary cutter
decorative wavy blade for a regular size rotary cutter (optional)

Preparing Your Background

1. Before you begin, steam press all of your fabrics and your batting to remove any wrinkles or creases. Then turn off the steam and use a hot iron for all of the fusing.

2. With an extra-fine-tip marker, trace the PETITE POPPIES pattern on pages 35–38 onto sheets of copy paper. (There's no need to include the labels on this master pattern.)

3. Tape the wrong sides of the traced sheets together to make your master pattern. You can also tape extra blank sheets around the outside of your master pattern to protect your ironing surface from stray bits of fusible web. Set the pattern aside for now (fig. 18).

Preparing Your Background and Design Pieces

1. Apply fusible web to the wrong sides of your background and border fabrics. Let the fabrics and fusible cool, then peel away the release paper (fig. 19).

18

2. Keep this release paper intact, because you will be using it throughout the process of creating your PETITE POPPIES quilt. Set aside the fused background and border fabrics for now.

Preparing Your Poppies

1. Now you will cut and assemble the design pieces for your poppies. Just in case you are tempted to fuse the design pieces to your background as you go, don't! As you will see later, there will be a specific order for fusing the design pieces to the background.

2. Let's start with the poppies (design pieces L, M, D, U, and N). Apply fusible web to the wrong sides of the fabrics you plan to use for your poppies. Let each fabric cool, but for now leave the release paper attached. As you will see in the next few steps, the order for tracing the design pieces—working from your lightest to darkest fabrics—is important.

19

3. Peel the release paper off the lightest poppy fabric (design pieces L). Place this sheet of release paper on top of your master pattern, and use an extra-fine-tip permanent marker to trace the design pieces L.

4. Place the release paper, ink side down, on the fusible side of your fabric. To protect your iron from any exposed fusible web, place an extra piece of release paper over the traced release paper and fabric (fig. 20). Press lightly with a hot iron to transfer the permanent ink to the back side of the fused fabric. Don't press for long—just long enough to transfer the marker to the fused fabric.

20

5. When you have the permanent ink transferred to your lightest fabric, set the fabric aside for the time being.

6. Before you trace the rest of your poppy design pieces (M, D, U, and N) keep in mind that you want the fabrics in each poppy to overlap just a bit. To prevent show through, you always want a darker fabric to overlap a lighter fabric. To get this overlap, you will trace just outside the pattern lines wherever the darker piece overlaps a lighter piece (fig. 21).

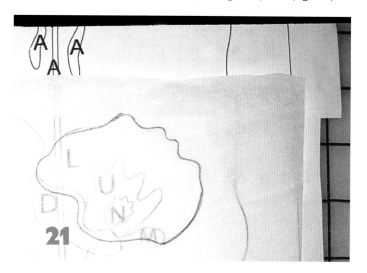
21

7. Peel the release paper off your medium fabric, and trace design pieces M from your master pattern onto the release paper. Make sure you trace slightly outside the lines wherever the design piece will need to overlap the lighter piece next to it.

8. Transfer the permanent ink from the release paper to your fabric, as described in step 4. Then trace and transfer design pieces D, U, and N to their respective fabrics.

If you are unsure how long to press, practice first on a test piece. You can always lift up a corner of the release paper, not peeling it all off, to see if the marker has transferred to the fabric. You do not want to overheat at this point as the fusible can get fused up!

Assembling your poppies

Now you will cut and assemble your poppy design pieces, using your traced pattern as a guide.

1. Place the sheet of release paper from the background fabric over your traced pattern.

2. Peel away the release papers from your poppy fabrics. (By removing the paper before cutting the pieces, you get a very clean crisp cut edge.) Cut the lightest pieces L, using very sharp small scissors. Be sure to trim all of the ink off the fabric. As you cut each piece, position it where it belongs on the traced pattern.

22

3. Cut the medium design pieces M and position them where they belong on the pattern. If needed, adjust the position of these pieces so they overlap the edges of the lightest pieces L by at least 1/16" (fig. 22).

4. Repeat step 3 for the remaining poppy design pieces. Leave your assembled poppies in place and cover them with release paper, and press lightly to fuse overlapping portions of the design pieces in each poppy.

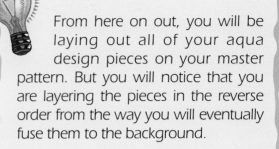

To cover your poppies, you can use the sheets of release paper you used from your poppy fabrics. There shouldn't be enough ink left on the sheets to transfer to your poppies. But to be on the safe side, you can place the sheets ink side up. The ink will not transfer to your iron in any case.

5. Set aside the background release paper and the fused poppies so you can trace the seed heads, buds, leaves, and curved stems from your master pattern.

Making your stems and leaves

1. Apply fusible web to the fabric you've chosen for your seed heads, buds, leaves, and stems. Let the fabric cool and peel off the release paper.

2. Trace the seed heads, buds, leaves, and curved stem pieces (but not the straight stems) on the release paper. You will make the straight stems by cutting them directly from the fabric. Be sure to trace these design pieces over to one side of the release paper so you will have at least 4" of fabric left for cutting the straight stems.

3. When you have finished tracing this last group of design pieces, position your fused poppies directly on the master pattern.

4. Place the ink side of the traced release paper to the fusible side of your leaf and stem fabric. Press lightly to transfer the traced lines from the release paper to the fabric the same way you did in step 4 on page 32.

From here on out, you will be laying out all of your aqua design pieces on your master pattern. But you will notice that you are layering the pieces in the reverse order from the way you will eventually fuse them to the background.

5. Remove the traced release paper. Cut the seed heads, buds, leaves, and curved stems, placing them on the master pattern to keep track of them as you go (fig. 23).

6. Place your remaining aqua fabric, fusible side up, on a cutting mat, and use an acrylic ruler to cut 11 strips 10" long. Make the strips 1/4" wide at one end and decrease the width at the other end.

7. Position the straight stems on your master pattern with the narrow ends at the top. Some of the strips will be longer than necessary, but you can leave them that way for now.

Fusing and Finishing Your PETITE POPPIES Design

Now for the fun—putting it all together into a quilt top! You will quilt as you go, alternating fusing the design pieces to your background and outline quilting them before adding the next layer of design pieces. Working from the bottom layer up allows easy access to the design pieces for outlining them and makes for a cleaner looking quilt.

1. Place your background fabric on a cutting mat with the fusible side up, and cut a piece 14½" x 16½" (about ½" larger than the finished quilt size).

2. Cut a piece of batting 15" x 17". Center your background fabric, fusible side down, on the batting. Cover this with the background release paper, and fuse the background to the batting.

3. Start by arranging the straight stem pieces on the background fabric, positioning them reasonably close to the way they are positioned in the PETITE POPPIES pattern. Trim off any excess from the bottom. Cover the straight stems with release paper and fuse them into place (fig. 24).

4. Cut a 14½" x 16½" piece of your border fabric and apply fusible web. Let the fabric cool and peel off the release paper. Center the release paper over your master pattern and trace the wavy outline around the design. Place the release paper, ink side down, on your border fabric and press to transfer the traced outline to the fabric.

5. Remove the release paper, and using very sharp small scissors or a rotary cutter, cut around the center shape to make a "frame" from your border fabric. Position the border around your PETITE POPPIES design and fuse it to the batting to complete your quilt top.

6. Cut 16" x 17" piece of your backing fabric. Place your quilt top on the backing and use safety pins to secure the outside and inside edges of the border. Then outline quilt the straight stems. You can quilt with a thread that matches your background or with colors that match the design piece being outlined. I always match my bobbin thread to my top thread.

7. The next layer of design pieces on your master pattern should be the leaves, curved stems, seed heads, and buds. Working across the design, fuse the leaves into place and outline quilt them. Then fuse the curved stems, seed heads, and buds in place and outline quilt them. Notice that one of the buds overlaps a poppy. Save this bud until after you have fused and outline quilted the poppies.

8. Fuse the poppies and the last bud in place, then outline quilt them. Outline stitch the border around its inner edge, then quilt the rest of the border and background with free-motion machine stitching (fig. 25).

9. Press the whole quilt top well with a hot iron and steam to make sure all the fused pieces are set. Use a rotary cutter to square up and trim the edges of the quilt, trimming it to 14" x 16". Add a hanging sleeve and a fused or sewn binding of your choice. Be sure to add a label to your quilt.

page 35   page 36

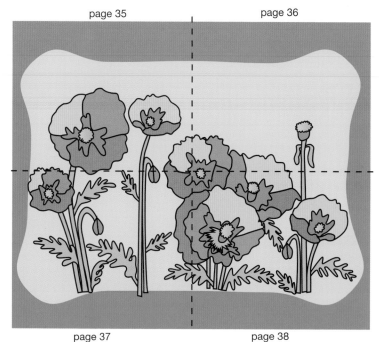

page 37   page 38

PETITE POPPIES **quilt assembly**

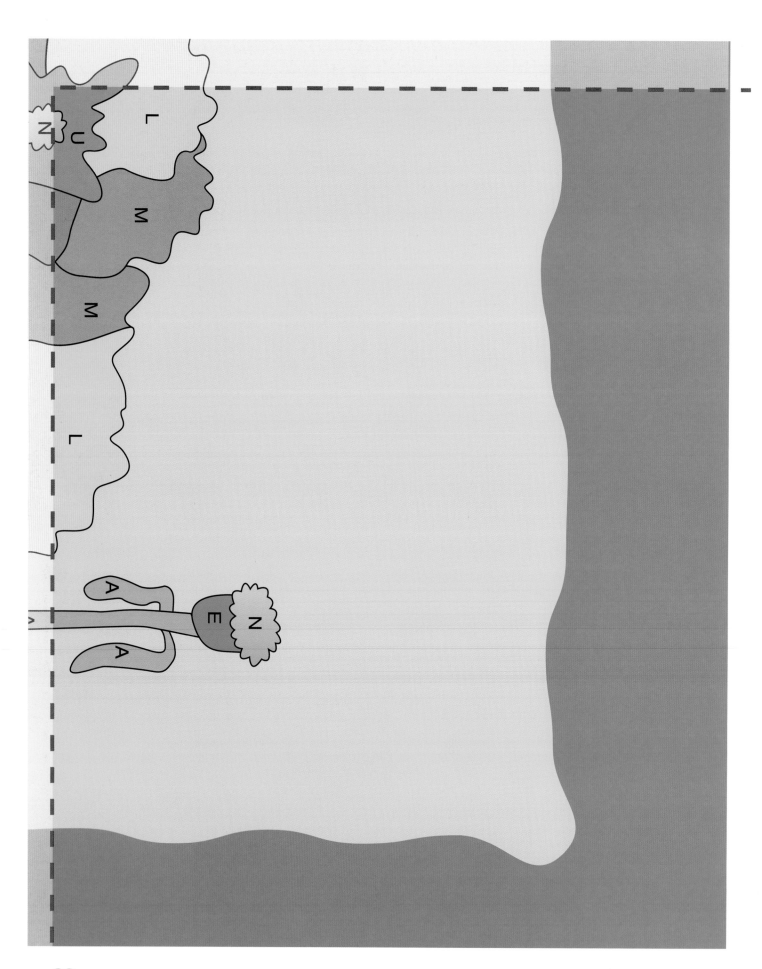

TULIPS, 15" x 20". Made by the author.

Standing tall and straight in my garden, surrounded by tiny little blue forget-me-nots, Tulips trumpet springs arrival. After a long winter their bright colors brighten the heart. They can brighten your heart everyday with this wonderful quilt on your wall.

Material	Amount

yellow/pink for background ....½ yd or 1 fat quarter

blue-green for border ....½ yd or 1 fat quarter

6 pairs of scraps (at least 3½" x 4½") for tulips (pieces T), each pair with 2 shades of various purples, lavenders, and pinks

aqua for the forget-me-not flowers (pieces F)

medium or dark green for tulip leaves (pieces D), ...¼ yd or 1 fat quarter

light green for forget-me-not leaves (pieces G) ....1 fat eighth or various scraps

yellow for forget-me-not centers (pieces J) ....1 fat eighth or scraps
or yellow embroidery thread for French knots (shown in photo)

fusible web ....2 yd

batting ....½ yd

backing.......................................1 fat quarter or ½ yd

binding ....¼ yd

you will also need: extra-fine-tip permanent marker
plain white copy paper 4–10 sheets
very sharp small scissors • rotary mat • rotary cutter
decorative wavy blade for a regular size rotary cutter

Preparing Your Master Pattern

1. With an extra-fine-tip marker, trace the TULIPS pattern on pages 43–46 onto sheets of copy paper. (There's no need to include the labels on this master pattern.)

2. Tape the wrong sides of the traced sheets together to make your master pattern. You can also tape extra blank sheets around the outside of your master pattern to protect your ironing surface from stray bits of fusible web. Set the pattern aside for now.

Preparing Your Background and Flowers

1. Before you begin, steam press all of your fabrics and your batting to remove any wrinkles or creases. Then turn off the steam and use a hot iron for all of the fusing.

2. Apply fusible web to the wrong side of your background

and border fabrics. Let the fabric and fusible web cool, then peel away the release paper.

3. Keep this release paper intact, because you will be using it throughout the process of creating your TULIPS quilt. Set aside the border fabrics for now.

Making your tulips

Now you will cut and assemble the design pieces for your tulips. Just in case you are tempted to fuse the design pieces to your background as you go, don't! As you will see later, there will be a specific order for fusing the design pieces to the background.

1. Apply fusible web to the wrong sides of the fabrics you plan to use for your tulips. Let the fabrics cool, then peel off the release papers. Place your tulip fabrics fusible side up on a rotary mat, and cut one piece 3½" x 4½" from each fabric.

2. Sort your fabrics into pairs of one lighter fabric and one darker fabric. Use a decorative wavy rotary blade to cut the 4½" dark edge in a slightly curving motion starting at the bottom and moving up (fig. 26). (You can practice this action on scraps first.)

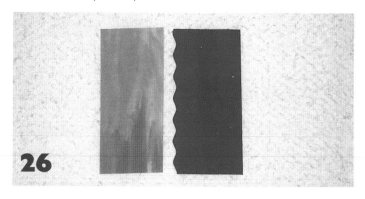

26

3. On a piece of release paper, place the wavy edge of the darker fabric over the lighter fabric, and lightly fuse them together. Repeat these steps for the remaining pairs of tulip fabrics.

4. With an extra-fine-tip permanent marker, trace each tulip from the master pattern onto a scrap of release paper. Center the traced tulips, ink side down, on the fusible side of the pairs of tulip fabrics. To protect your iron from any exposed fusible web, place an extra piece of release paper over the traced release paper and fabric. Press lightly with a hot iron to transfer the permanent ink to the back side of the fused fabric. Don't press for long--just long enough to transfer the marker to the fused fabric.

5. Peel the release paper off your tulip fabrics and use very sharp small scissors to cut out the tulips. Be sure to trim all of the ink off the lighter fabrics (fig. 27). Set your tulips aside for now.

27

If you are unsure how long to press, practice first on a test piece. You can always lift up a corner of the release paper, not peeling it all off, to see if the marker has transferred to the fabric. You do not want to overheat at this point as the fusible can get fused up!

Making the forget-me-nots

1. On scraps of release paper, trace the leaves (piece G) for the forget-me-nots. Trace each three-leaf cluster as a single unit.

2. Transfer the ink from the release paper to the fusible side of your leaf fabric as you did in step 4, on page 40. Remove the release paper and cut out your leaves. Place them on the release paper with your tulips.

3. Trace and cut out the forget-me-nots and their yellow centers. Place the flowers and centers over their leaves on the release paper, and lightly fuse each one. You can add yellow embroidered French knots later in place of the yellow centers.

4. Begin laying out your design on a piece of release paper, positioning the tulips and forget-me-nots according to the quilt assembly diagram on page 42.

Making your tulip stems and leaves

1. Apply fusible web to the fabric you've chosen for your tulip leaves and stems. Let the fabric cool and peel off the release paper.

2. Rotary cut five straight stems 11" long and a little more than ⅛" wide. Set these straight stems aside for now.

3. Trace the tulip leaves and the curved stem onto the release paper. Transfer the leaf tracings to your leaf fabric, cut out the leaves, and put them on the release paper on top of your tulips and forget-me-nots (fig. 28).

28

4. Now add the straight stems to the design, but don't trim their lengths yet.

Fusing and Finishing Your TULIPS Design

Now for the fun—putting it all together into a quilt top! You will quilt as you go, alternating fusing the design pieces to your background and outline quilting them before adding the next layer of design pieces. Working from the bottom layer up allows easy access to the design pieces for outline quilting them and makes for a cleaner looking quilt.

1. Place the background fabric on a cutting mat with the fusible side up, and cut a piece 15½" x 20½" (about ½" larger than the finished quilt size). Cut the same size rectangle from your border fabric.

2. Center a piece of release paper from over your master pattern and trace the wavy outline around the design. Place the release paper, ink side down, on your border fabric and press to transfer the traced outline to the fabric.

3. Remove the release paper, and using very sharp small scissors or a rotary cutter, cut around the center shape to make a "frame" from your border fabric. Position the border around your TULIPS design and fuse it to the batting to complete your quilt top.

4. Cut a piece of batting 16" x 21". Center your background and border, fusible side down, on the batting, and fuse the background to the batting.

5. Start by arranging the straight stem pieces on the background fabric according to the quilt assembly diagram. Trim off any excess from the bottoms of the stems.

6. Cover the straight stems with release paper and fuse them into place. Then outline quilt the stems.

7. The next layer of design pieces on your master pattern should be the tulip leaves and the curved stem. Working across the design, fuse the leaves and curved stem into place and outline quilt them.

8. Fuse the tulips and forget-me-nots to your background and outline quilt them. Outline quilt the border around its

inner edge, then quilt the rest of the border and background with free-motion machine stitching (fig. 29).

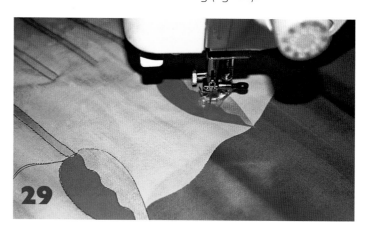

29

9. Press the whole quilt top well with a hot iron and steam to make sure all the fused pieces are set. Use a rotary cutter to square up and trim the edges of the quilt, trimming it to 15" x 20". Embroider yellow French knots for the flower centers shown in the quilt on page 39. Add a hanging sleeve and a fused or sewn binding of your choice. Be sure to add a label to your quilt.

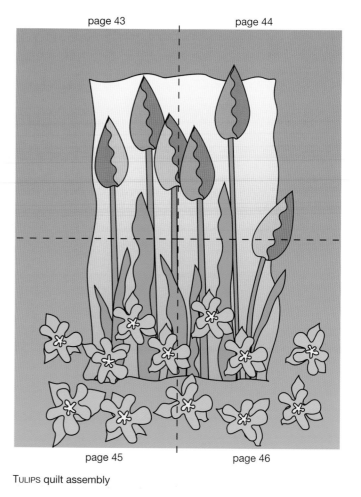

page 43   page 44

page 45   page 46

TULIPS quilt assembly

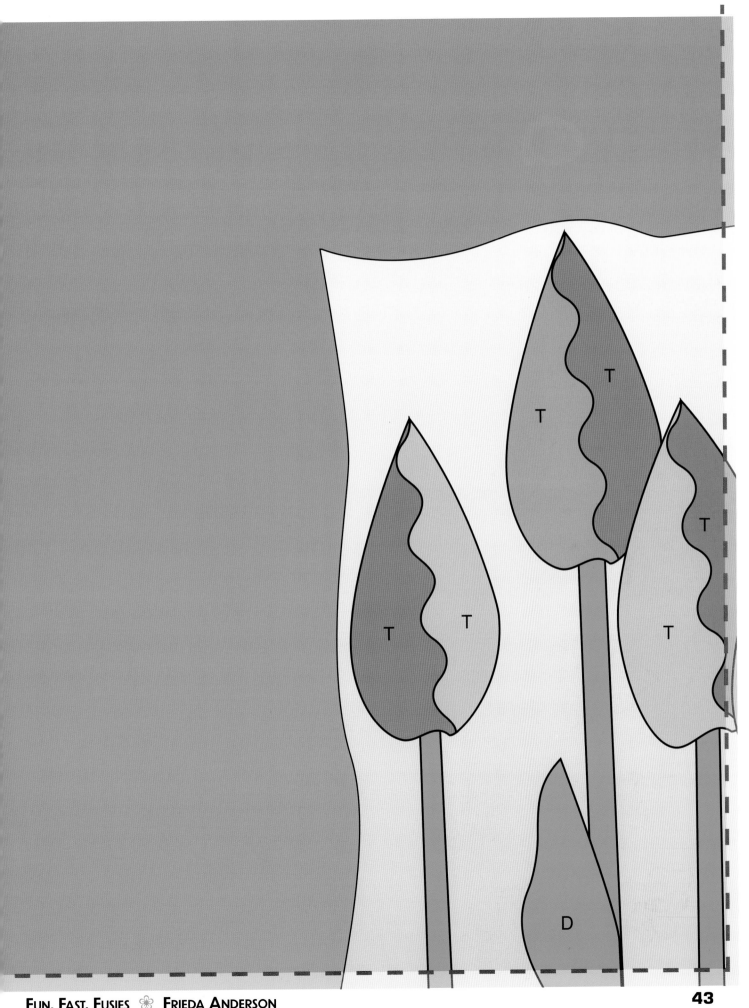

Dandelions

DANDELIONS, 15" x 20". Made by the author.

I believe that dandelions deserve more respect. They are so happy, bright, and cheerful, I had to give them their own quilt.

Material	Amount
purple/pink for background	1 fat quarter
fuchsia/orange for border	1 fat quarter
bright yellow (piece Y)	scraps or 1 fat eighth
medium yellow (piece M)	scraps or 1 fat eighth
pale yellow (piece P)	scraps or 1 fat eighth
medium green (piece G)	scraps or 1 fat eighth
dark green (piece K)	scraps or 1 fat eighth
light green (piece L)	scraps or 1 fat eighth
fusible web	3 yd
batting	17" X 21"
backing	¾ yd
binding	½ yd

you will also need: extra-fine-tip permanent marker
plain white copy paper, 4–10 sheets
very sharp small scissors • rotary mat • rotary cutter
decorative wavy blade for a rotary cutter

Preparing Your Master Pattern

1. Before you begin, steam press all of your fabrics and your batting to remove any wrinkles or creases. Then turn off the steam and use a hot iron for all of the fusing.

2. With an extra-fine-tip marker, trace the DANDELIONS pattern on pages 51–54 onto sheets of copy paper. (There's no need to include the labels on this master pattern).

3. Tape the wrong sides of the traced sheets together to make your master pattern. You can also tape extra blank sheets around the outside of your master pattern to protect your ironing surface from stray bits of fusible web. Set the pattern aside for now.

Preparing Your Background and Border

1. Apply fusible web to the wrong sides of your background and border fabrics. Let the fabrics and fusible cool, then peel away the release paper. Keep this release paper intact, because you will be using it throughout the process of creating your DANDELIONS quilt

2. Place your background fabric on a cutting mat with the fusible side up, and cut a rectangle 15½" x 16½" (about ½" larger than the finished quilt size). Cut the same size rectangle from your border fabric.

3. Center a piece of release paper over your master pattern and trace the wavy line that forms the inner edge of the border.

4. Place the release paper, ink side down, on the fusible side of your border fabric. Press lightly with a hot iron to transfer the permanent ink to the back side of the fused fabric. Don't press for long—just long enough to transfer the marker to the fused fabric.

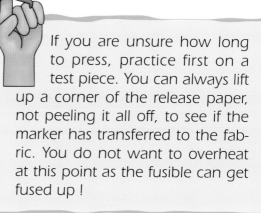

If you are unsure how long to press, practice first on a test piece. You can always lift up a corner of the release paper, not peeling it all off, to see if the marker has transferred to the fabric. You do not want to overheat at this point as the fusible can get fused up !

5. Remove the release paper, and using very sharp small scissors or a rotary cutter, cut around the wavy line to make a "frame" from your border fabric. Position the border over the background fabric and lightly fuse the border to the background.

6. Cut a piece of batting 16" x 21". Center your background and border, fusible side down, on the batting. Cover this with the background release paper, and fuse the background and border to the batting (fig. 30).

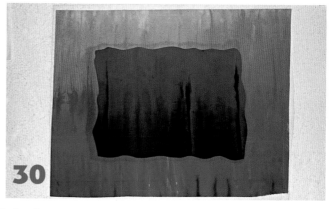

30

7. Outline quilt your border just inside its inner wavy edge.

Preparing Your Leaves and Dandelions

Now you will assemble elements of your DANDELIONS design, beginning with the leaves. Just in case you are tempted to fuse the design pieces to your background as you go, don't! As you will see later, there will be a specific order for fusing the design pieces to the background.

Transferring the design pieces to your fabric

1. Apply fusible web to your leaf and dandelion fabrics. Leave the release paper attached to the fabric for now. Let each fabric cool, but leave the release paper attached until you are ready to trace the designs onto each piece.

2. Peel the release paper off your light green fabric (pieces L). Trace the bud stems, and trace each leaf labeled L on your master pattern. Be sure to trace the whole leaf outline. Right next to your tracing, but not inside it, mark the leaf number L2, L3, and so on. Since the leaves are so similar in shape, later on these numbers will help you keep track of which leaf is which. Transfer the ink tracings to your light green fabric, as described in step 4 on page 48. (Don't cut out the leaves just yet.)

3. On your dark and medium green fabrics, trace and transfer whole leaf outlines for pieces G and K. Mark the leaf numbers as you did in step 2 above. Then transfer the leaf tracings to your fabrics.

4. Trace and transfer the dandelion pieces Y, M, and P to their respective yellow fabrics.

Assembling your leaves and dandelions

Now you will cut and assemble your dandelion design pieces, using your traced pattern as a guide.

1. Remove the release paper from the dark fabric (K) and the light fabric (L) for leaf L1. Place the dark piece on a rotary mat, fusible side up, and trim one side with a wavy rotary blade (fig. 31).

2. On a piece of release paper, place the wavy edge of the darker fabric over the lighter fabric and lightly fuse them.

3. Place the release paper with the outline of leaf L1 inkside down on the fusible side of the web and press lightly to

transfer the ink to the back of the fused fabrics. With small, sharp scissors, cut out leaf L1 (fig 32).

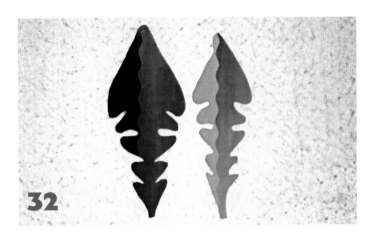

4. Start laying out your design by placing this leaf on top of leaf L1 on your master pattern. Continue cutting out and assembling the two-toned leaves L2–L9, and lay them out on your master pattern as you go (fig. 33).

5. Cut the remaining leaves L10–L16 and add them to the layout on your master pattern.

6. Cut and assemble the dandelions and buds from your yellow fabrics. Lightly fuse the dandelion pieces together. Set the dandelions aside for now.

Fusing and Quilting Your DANDELIONS Design

Now for the fun—putting it all together into a quilt top! You will quilt as you go, alternating fusing the design pieces to your background and outline quilting them before adding the next layer of design pieces. Working from the bottom layer up allows easy access to the design pieces for outlining them and makes for a cleaner looking quilt.

1. Starting in the center of the design, place leaves 1–9 on your background fabric, according to the quilt assembly diagram. Fuse the leaves into place and outline quilt them.

2. Fuse the dandelions and buds then outline quilt them. Then quilt the rest of the border and background with free-motion machine stitching.

3. Press the whole quilt top well with a hot iron and steam to make sure all the fused pieces are set. Use a rotary cutter to square up and trim the edges of the quilt, trimming it to 15" x 20". Add a hanging sleeve and a fused or sewn binding of your choice. Be sure to add a label to your quilt.

page 51   page 52

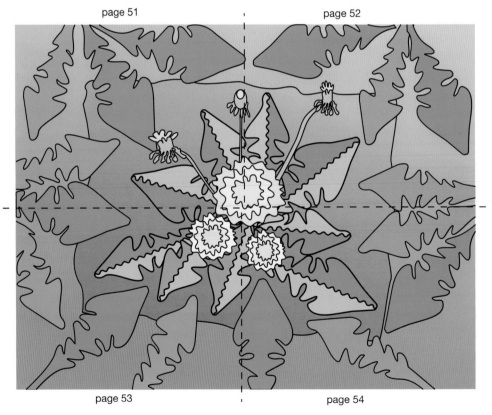

page 53   page 54

DANDELIONS **quilt assembly**

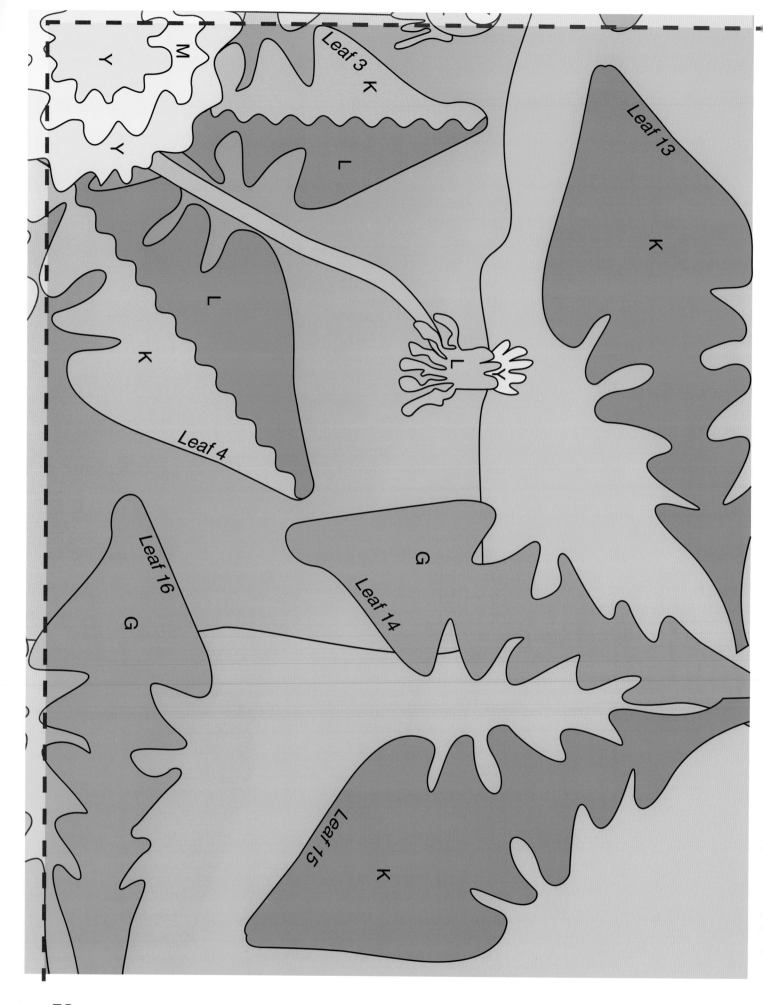

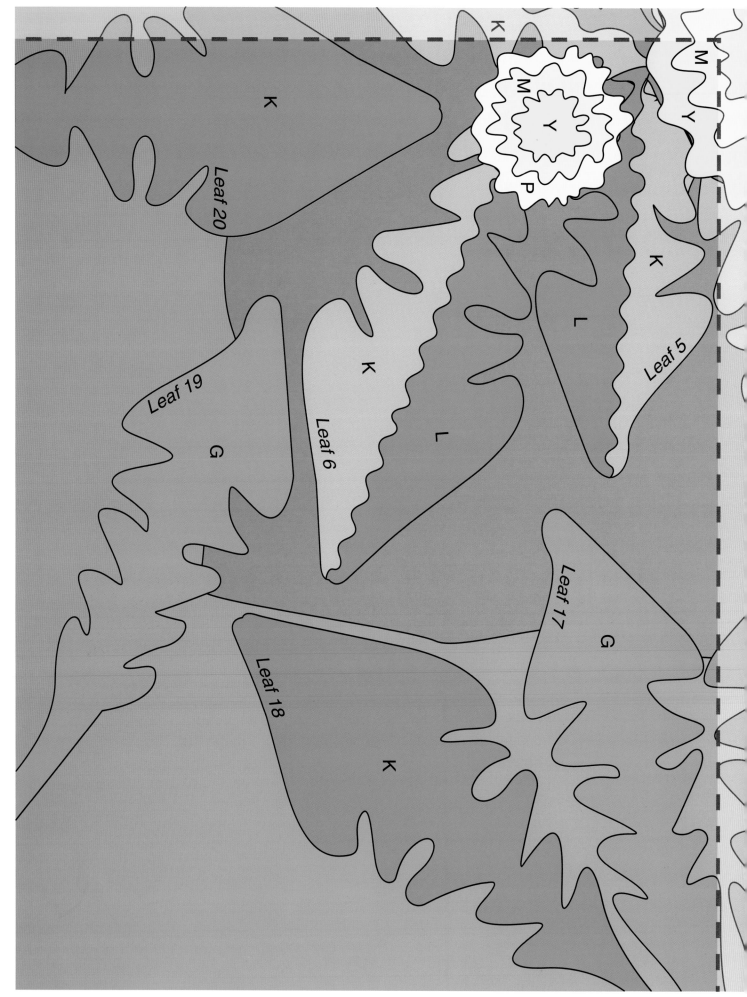

Pears

Pears, 15" x 30". Made by the author.

Fruit, fruit, fruit—we all need a little fruit each day. The background and border in this quilt echo the curving shapes of the pears. The layers of green that harmonize against the lavender setting give each pear its own shaping. The warmth of the red/rust border brings to mind the changing colors of an autumn day.

Material	Amount
purple for background	½ yd
rust for border	½ yd
dark green and pale for leaves and pears (pieces A and B)	1 fat eighth each
5 shades of greens and yellow-greens for pears (pieces C, D, E, F, and G)	1 fat eighth each
fusible web	2 yd
batting	½ yd
backing	½ yd
binding	½ yd

you will also need: extra-fine-tip permanent marker
plain white copy paper, 4–10 sheets
very sharp small scissors • rotary mat • rotary cutter

Preparing the Pears and Leaves

You will begin by cutting and assembling groups of design pieces for your pears and leaves. Just in case you are tempted to fuse the design pieces to your background as you go, don't! As you will see later, there will be a specific order for fusing the design pieces to the background.

Making a master pattern

1. With an extra-fine-tip marker, trace the PEARS pattern on pages 58 and 59 onto sheets of copy paper. Be sure to write in the labels on your master pattern.

2. Tape the wrong sides of the traced sheets together to make your master pattern. You can also tape extra blank sheets around the outside of your master pattern to protect your ironing surface from stray bits of fusible web. Set the pattern aside for now.

Tracing the design pieces

1. Before you begin, steam press all of your fabrics and your batting to remove any wrinkles or creases. Then turn off the steam and use a hot iron for all of the fusing.

2. Apply fusible web to your purple background fabric and rust border fabric. Let the fabrics and fusible cool, then peel the release paper off both fabrics. Set the fabrics aside for now, but keep the release papers handy.

3. Decide which fabrics you will use for each design piece, A though G. In one corner of each fabric, write the letter assigned to that design piece. To help you keep track of which fabric corresponds to which label in the pattern, snip off the labeled corners and tape them to an index card. You can use this card as a reference as you work.

4. Apply fusible web to the wrong sides of the fabrics you have selected for the pears and leaves. Let each fabric cool, but for now leave the release paper attached until you are ready to use the fabric.

5. Peel the release paper off fabric A. Place this paper on top of your master pattern, and use an extra-fine-tip permanent marker to trace all of the design pieces labeled A. To help keep track of all these little odd-shaped pieces as you cut them out, group and label them according to the design element they belong to, such as Leaf 1, Pear 1, and so on.

6. Place the release paper with the tracings of design pieces A, ink side down, on the fusible side of your fabric A. To protect your iron from any exposed fusible web, place an extra piece of release paper over the traced release paper and fabric. Press lightly with a hot iron to transfer the permanent ink to the back side of the fused fabric. Don't press for long—just long enough to transfer the marker to the fused fabric.

If you are unsure how long to press, practice first on a test piece. You can always lift up a corner of the release paper, not peeling it all off, to see if the marker has transferred to the fabric. You do not want to overheat at this point as the fusible can get fused up!

7. When you have the permanent ink transferred to your fabric A, set it aside and repeat steps 5 and 6 for the rest of your fabrics, B through G (fig. 34, page 57).

34

Assembling the design elements

1. Let's start with the pear on the left (design element Pear 1). Peel the release paper off your fabrics. By removing the paper before cutting, you get a very clean crisp cut edge. Cut the design pieces for Pear 1, using very sharp small scissors.

2. Layer the design pieces for your first pear, fusible side down, on top of the release paper from your background fabric, according to the quilt assembly diagram. You don't have to be exact. Just eyeball the placement of the pieces and adjust their positions according to what looks good to you.

3. When the pear looks right to you, cover it with another piece of release paper and lightly fuse the layers together to create one unit.

4. Repeat these steps to make the other two pears in the design. Then make the leaves in the same way. Set aside the release paper with the fused pears and leaves (fig. 35).

35

Fusing and Finishing Your Pears Design

Now for the fun—putting it all together into a quilt top!

1. Place your background fabric on a cutting mat with the fusible side up, and cut a piece 8" x 15½" (about ½" larger than the finished quilt size). Cut a piece of border fabric and one piece of release paper 8" x 15½".

2. Center the release paper over your master pattern and trace the wavy outline around the design. Place the release paper, ink side down, on your border fabric and press to transfer the traced outline to the fabric.

3. Remove the release paper, and using very sharp small scissors or a rotary cutter, cut around the outlined shape to make a "frame" from your border fabric. Lightly fuse the border to your background fabric.

4. Cut a piece of batting 8½" x 16". Center your background and border, fusible side down, on the batting. Cover this with release paper, and fuse the background and border to the batting.

5. Position your pears and leaves on the background and border according to the quilt assembly diagram.

6. Outline stitch the pears and leaves. Outline quilt around the inner edge of the border, then quilt the rest of the border and background with free-motion machine stitching.

7. Press the whole quilt top well with a hot iron and steam to make sure all the fused pieces are set. Use a rotary cutter to square up and trim the edges of the quilt, trimming it to 7½" x 15". Add a hanging sleeve and a fused or sewn binding of your choice. Be sure to add a label to your quilt.

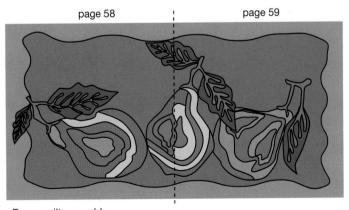

page 58   page 59

PEARS **quilt assembly**

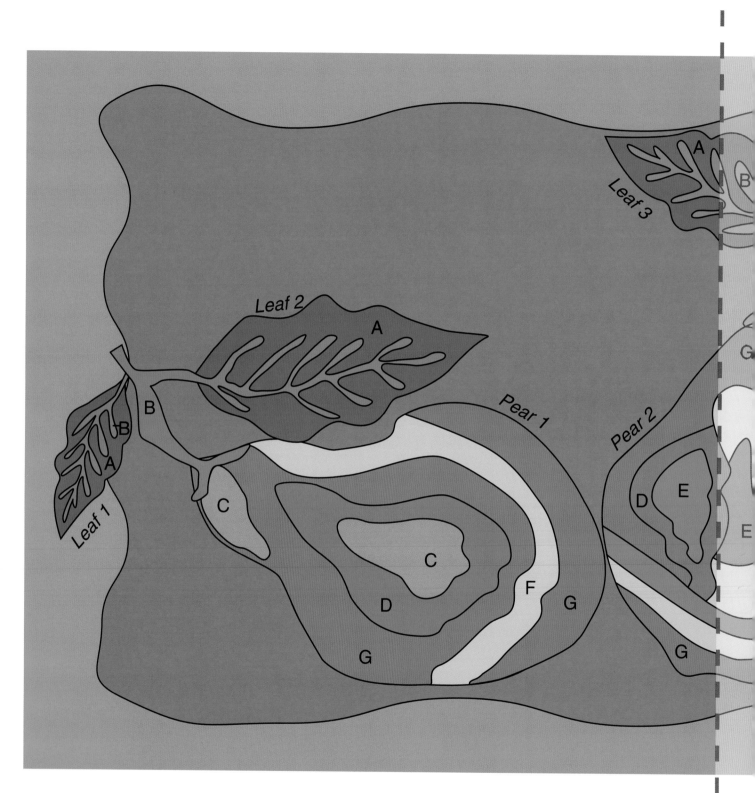

To make this quilt the same size as the author's,
you can enlarge this pattern 200%.

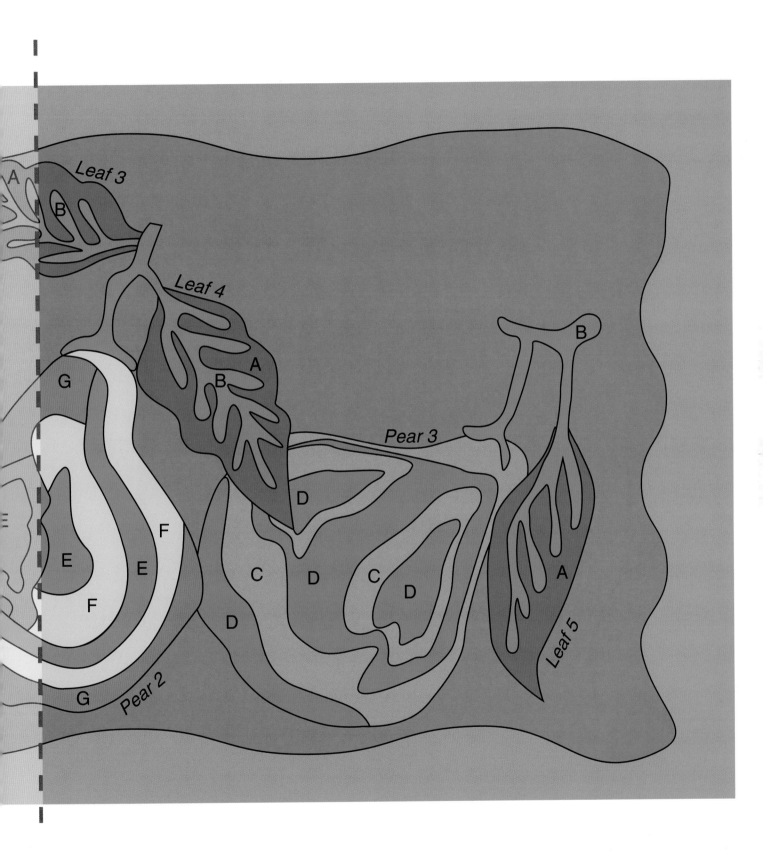

Sunflowers

SUNFLOWERS, 15" x 20". Made by the author.

Sunflowers are one of the few major flowers that originated in the United States. *Helianthus* comes from the Greek for sun and flower. If you watch it during the day, it turns its head to follow the sun.

Material	Amount
aqua for background	1 fat quarter
light green, for inner border and leaf veins (pieces L)	1 fat quarter
orange/yellow for outer border	1 fat quarter
yellow for flower petals (pieces Y)	1 fat quarter
medium green, for leaves and stems (pieces M)	1 fat eighth
dark green, for leaves and stems (pieces D)	1 fat eighth
dark orange for flower centers (pieces O)	1 fat quarter
rust for sunflower centers (pieces R)	1 fat quarter
orange for sunflower centers (pieces N)	1 fat eighth
fusible web	2 yd
batting	½ yd
backing	½ yd
binding	½ yard

you will also need: extra-fine-tip permanent marker
plain white copy paper, 4–10 sheets
very sharp small scissors • rotary mat • rotary cutter

Preparing Your Master Pattern

1. With an extra-fine-tip marker, trace the SUNFLOWER pattern on pages 64–67 onto sheets of copy paper. (There's no need to include the labels on this master pattern.)

2. Tape the wrong sides of the traced sheets together to make your master pattern. You can also tape extra blank sheets around the outside of your master pattern to protect your ironing surface from stray bits of fusible web. Set the pattern aside for now.

Preparing Your Background and Borders

1. Before you begin, steam press all of your fabrics and your batting to remove any wrinkles or creases. Then turn off the steam and use a hot iron for all of the fusing.

2. Apply fusible web to the wrong side of your background fabric. Let the fabric and fusible cool. Place the background fabric on a cutting mat with the fusible side up, and cut a piece 12¾" x 14¼".

3. Let the fabric and fusible web cool, then peel away the release paper. Keep this release paper intact, because you will be using it throughout the process of creating your quilt.

4. Cut a 15½" x 20½" piece of your light green inner border fabric (about ½" overall larger than the finished quilt), and apply fusible web. Let the fabric cool and peel off the release paper. Center the release paper over your master pattern and trace the inner wavy line in the design.

5. Place the release paper, ink side down, on the fusible side of your fabric. To protect your iron from any exposed fusible web, place an extra piece of release paper over the traced release paper and fabric. Press lightly with a hot iron to transfer the permanent ink to the back side of the fused fabric. Don't press for long—just long enough to transfer the marker to the fused fabric.

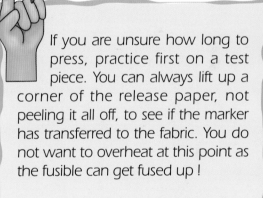

If you are unsure how long to press, practice first on a test piece. You can always lift up a corner of the release paper, not peeling it all off, to see if the marker has transferred to the fabric. You do not want to overheat at this point as the fusible can get fused up !

6. Remove the release paper, and with very sharp small scissors or a rotary cutter, cut around the wavy line to make an inner "frame" from your inner border fabric. Make sure to trim all of the ink off the light fabric.

7. Place your background piece on release paper, position the inner border piece on top of it, and fuse the border to the background.

8. Cut a 15½" x 20½" piece of your outer border fabric and apply fusible web. Let the fabric cool and peel off the release paper. Center the release paper over your master pattern and trace the outer wavy line in the design (fig. 36, page 62).

9. Transfer the ink to your outer border fabric as you did in step 5 on page 61. Cut along the wavy line to create an outer frame and fuse this piece to the light green inner border.

10. Cut a piece of batting 16" x 21". Center your background and border piece on the batting and fuse everything together.

36

Making Sunflowers and Leaves

Now you will cut and assemble the design pieces for your sunflowers. Just in case you are tempted to fuse the design pieces to your background as you go, don't! As you will see later, there will be a specific order for fusing the design pieces to the background.

Preparing the design pieces

1. Apply fusible web to the fabrics you plan to use for your sunflower and leaf design pieces. Let each fabric cool, but for now leave the release paper attached.

2. Peel the release paper off the yellow fabric you plan to use for the sunflowers. Trace the design pieces Y from your master pattern onto the release paper. (As shown with the dashed lines on the sunflowers, you will "draw" the individual petals when you quilt the sunflowers.)

3. Transfer the permanent ink from the release paper to your fabric, as described in step 5 on page 61. Then trace and transfer the remaining design pieces to their respective fabrics.

Assembling your sunflowers

Now you will cut and assemble your sunflower design pieces, using your traced pattern as a guide.

1. Place a sheet of release paper over your traced pattern. Peel away the release papers from your sunflower petal fabrics Y. (By removing the paper before cutting the pieces, you get a very clean crisp cut edge.) Cut out the sunflowers using very sharp small scissors. Be sure to trim all of the ink off the fabric. As you cut each piece, position it where it belongs on the traced pattern (fig. 37).

2. Cut sunflower centers (design pieces R, O, and N) and position them where they belong on the pattern.

3. Leave your assembled sunflowers in place. Cover them with release paper, and press lightly to fuse overlapping portions of the design pieces in each sunflower.

37

4. Set aside the background release paper and the fused sunflowers so you can trace the leaves and stems. Repeat steps 1 through 3 to cut and assemble the sunflower leaves and stems (design pieces L, M, and D) (fig. 38, page 63).

38

Fusing and Finishing Your Sunflowers Design

Now for the fun—putting it all together into a quilt top! You will quilt as you go, alternating fusing the design pieces to your background and outline quilting them before adding the next layer of the design. Working from the bottom layer up allows easy access to the design pieces for outlining them and makes for a cleaner looking quilt.

1. Start by arranging the stems on the background fabric, positioning them reasonably close to the way they are positioned in the SUNFLOWERS quilt assembly diagram on the right. Cover the straight stems with release paper and fuse them into place.

2. Cut a 16½" x 21½" piece of your backing fabric. Place your quilt top on the backing and use safety pins to secure the edges. Then outline quilt the stems. You can quilt with a

thread that matches your background or with colors that match the design piece being outlined. I always match my bobbin thread to my top thread.

3. The next layer of design pieces on your master pattern should be the leaves. Working across the design, fuse the leaves into place and outline quilt them. Then fuse and outline quilt the sunflowers.

4. Press the whole quilt top well with a hot iron and steam to make sure all the fused pieces are set. Use a rotary cutter to square up and trim the edges of the quilt, trimming it to 15" x 20". Add a hanging sleeve and a fused or sewn binding of your choice. Be sure to add a label to your quilt.

page 64 | page 65

page 66 | page 67

SUNFLOWERS **quilt assembly**

Dashes in flowers indicate decorative quilting lines.

inner background cutting line

Sunflower 1

D

M

Y

M

L

R

N

M

M

L

D

M

Sunflower 3

Y

R

L

M

L

M

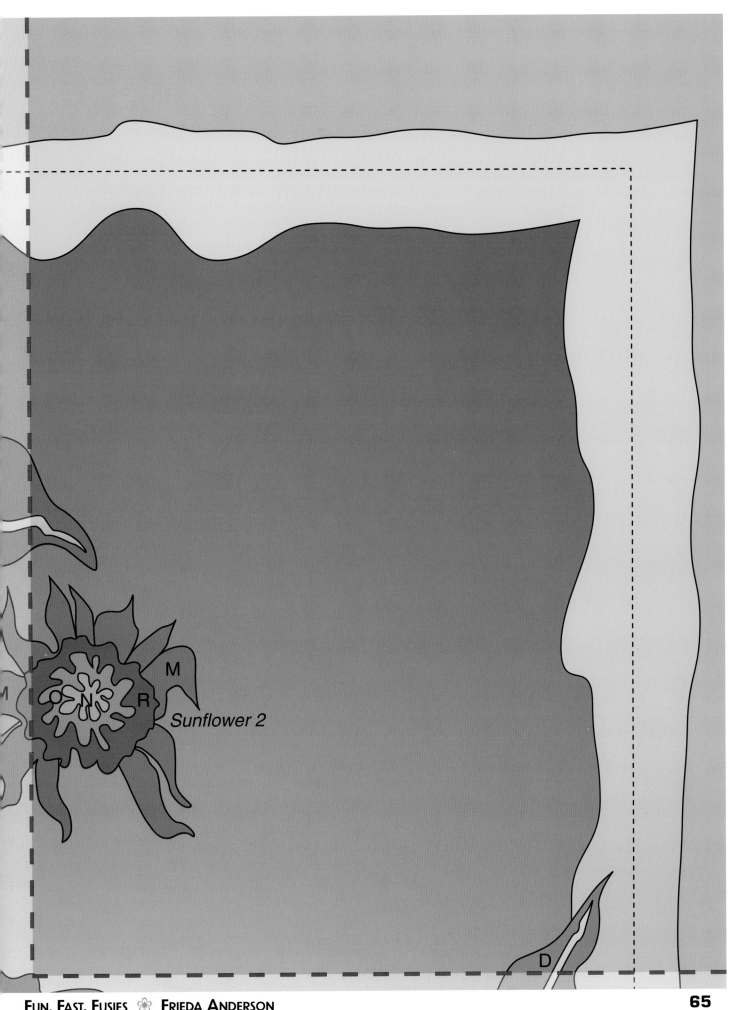

Sunflower 2

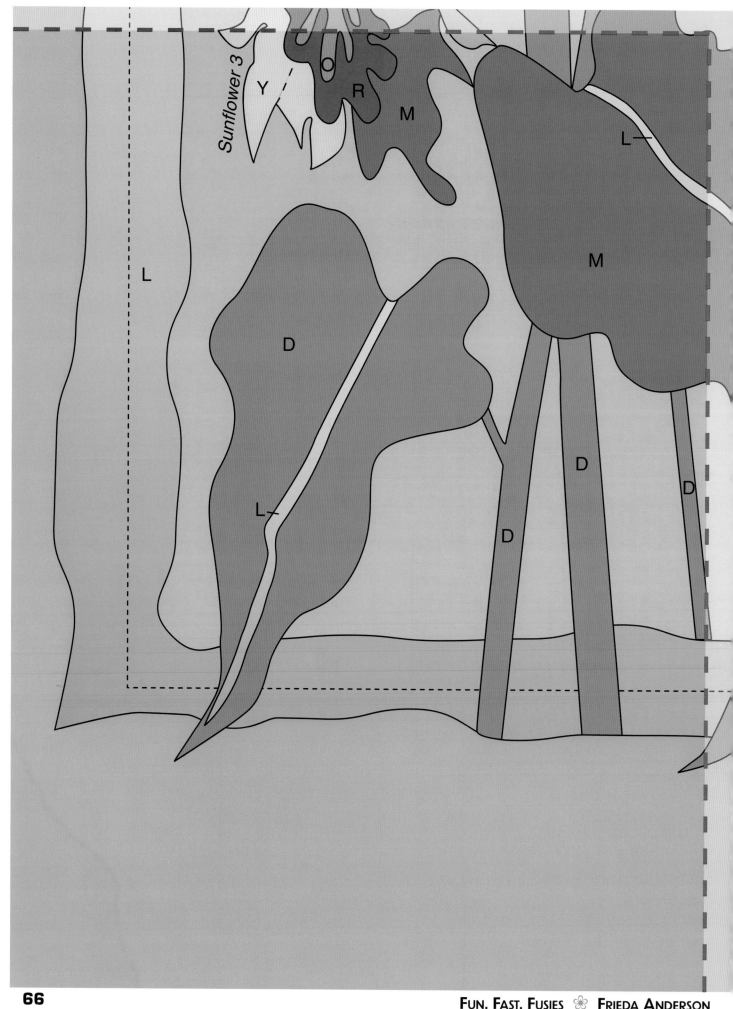

Sunflower 3

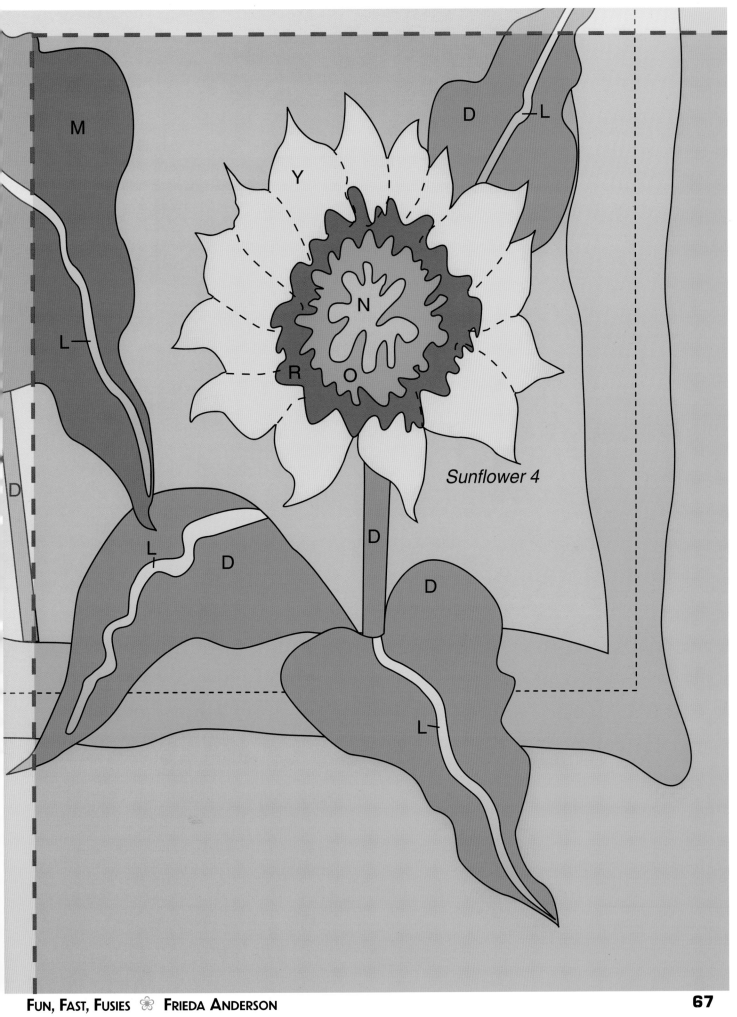

Sunflower 4

FALL TREE, 15" x 20". Made by the author.

In the fall, as I walk in the woods near my home, the colors call to me. I find the colors of fall warm and peaceful, relaxing my mind and preparing me for the solitude of winter to come.

Material	Amount
mustard yellow for background ...½ yd or 1 fat quarter	
rust for border ....½ yd	
mud brown or mud green for tree ....1 fat quarter	
dark oranges, browns, purples, and rust for leaves ....scraps or 1 fat eighth of each	
darker mud orange or brown for forest floor ....1 fat eighth of each (I used one of my striped hand-dyed fabrics.)	
fusible web ....3 yd	
batting ....21" X 16"	
backing...¾ yd	
binding ....½ yd	

you will also need: extra-fine-tip permanent marker
plain white copy paper, 4–10 sheets
very sharp small scissors ▪ rotary mat ▪ rotary cutter
decorative wavy blade for a regular size rotary cutter

Preparing Your Master Pattern

1. Before you begin, steam press all of your fabrics and your batting to remove any wrinkles or creases. Then turn off the steam and use a hot iron for all of the fusing.

2. With an extra-fine-tip marker, trace the FALL TREE pattern on pages 72–75 onto sheets of copy paper.

3. Tape the wrong sides of the traced sheets together to make your master pattern. You can also tape extra blank sheets around the outside of your master pattern to protect your ironing surface from stray bits of fusible web. Set the pattern aside for now.

Preparing Your Background and Border

1. Apply fusible web to the wrong sides of your mustard-yellow and mud-orange background, and rust border fabrics. Let the fabrics and fusible cool, then peel away the release paper. Keep this release paper intact, because you will be using it throughout the process of creating your FALL TREE quilt.

2. Place your mustard-yellow background fabric on a cutting mat with the fusible side up, and cut a rectangle 12½" x 13".

3. Cut a rectangle 12" x 6" from the mud-orange fabric that you plan to use for the dirt under the tree. Trim one of the 10½" sides to give it a slant, as shown in the quilt assembly diagram on page 71.

4. Cut a piece of batting 21" x 16". Center the background and mud-orange fabrics on the batting, and lightly fuse everything together (fig. 39).

39

5. Cut a rectangle 20½" x 15½" from your fused border fabric. Center a piece of release paper over your master pattern and trace the wavy line that forms the inner edge of the border.

6. Place the release paper, ink side down, on the fusible side of your border fabric. Press lightly with a hot iron to transfer the permanent ink to the back side of the fused fabric. Don't press for long—just long enough to transfer the marker to the fused fabric.

If you are unsure how long to press, practice first on a test piece. You can always lift up a corner of the release paper, not peeling it all off, to see if the marker has transferred to the fabric. You do not want to overheat at this point as the fusible can get fused up!

7. Remove the release paper, and using very sharp small scissors or a rotary cutter, cut around the wavy line to make a "frame" from your border fabric. Position the border over the background fabric and lightly fuse the border to the background.

8. Center your border, fusible side down, on top of the background and batting. Cover this with the background release paper, and fuse everything together (fig.40).

40

9. Cut a 21½" x 16½" piece of your backing fabric. Place your background and batting on the backing and use safety pins to secure the outside and inside edges of the border.

10. Outline quilt your border just inside its inner wavy edge. You can quilt with a thread that matches your background or with colors that match the design piece being outlined. I always match my bobbin thread to my top thread.

Making Your Tree and Leaves

1. On a sheet of release paper, trace the tree with a fine-point permanent marker. Using a small ruler helps keep the lines straight.

2. Transfer the ink tracing to your tree fabric, and cut out the tree. You can use a tiny 18mm rotary cutter and blade along with an acrylic ruler to cut the straight lines, then use very sharp embroidery scissors in the tight inside corners.

3. Place the tree on your background with the roots positioned on the forest floor portion of the background. Fuse the tree to the background, and outline quilt it.

4. Trace the solid outlines of the 17 leaves. Choose fabrics for the three leaves under the tree. Transfer the tracings of the three leaves to your fabrics, cut them out, and position them around the roots of the tree. Don't fuse them just yet. Wait until you have all of the leaves placed so you can adjust their positions as desired.

5. Choose two fabrics for each of the 14 leaves, 12 around the upper part of the tree and two under the tree. To make one leaf, transfer one leaf tracing to the lighter of the two fabrics. Do this for all 14 leaves

6. Stack the two fabrics in the same direction, right sides down, and cut out the pair together.

7. Separate a pair of leaves and trim about ⅛" off the left side of one leaf in the pair. Do this for six pairs of leaves. You will use the trimmed pieces around the bottom of the tree (fig. 41).

41

8. Separate a pair of leaves and trim about ⅛" off the right side of one leaf in the pair. Do this for six pairs of leaves. You will use the trimmed pieces around the bottom border under the tree.

Fusing and Quilting Your Fall Tree Design

Now for the fun—putting it all together into a quilt top!

1. Arrange your leaves around the outside of the tree as shown in the quilt assembly diagram. Arrange the trimmed pieces around the bottom of the tree as shown.

2. Fuse the leaves to the quilt top and outline quilt them.

3. Press the whole quilt top well with a hot iron and steam to make sure all the fused pieces are set. Use a rotary cutter to square up and trim the edges of the quilt, trimming it to 20" x 15". Add a hanging sleeve and a fused or sewn binding of your choice. Be sure to add a label to your quilt.

page 72   page 73

page 74   page 75

FALL TREE quilt assembly

74

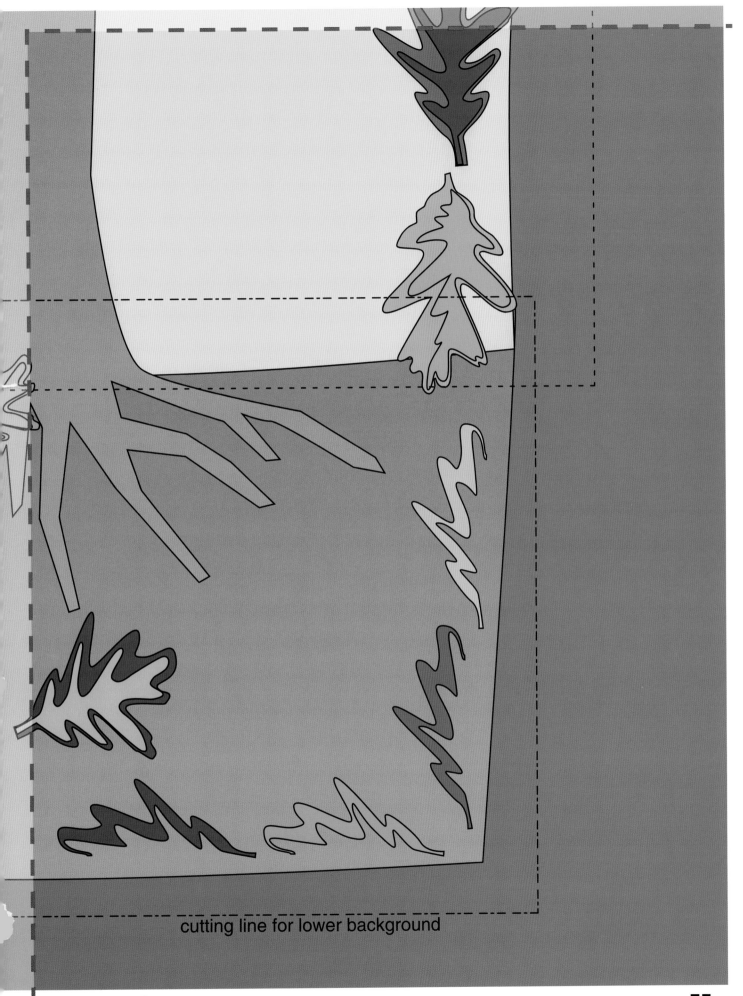

cutting line for lower background

Organic Leaves

ORGANIC LEAVES, 15" x 15". Made by the author.

The idea for this quilt came from the carpet of fall leaves along the path where I take one of my daily walks. I call this quilt ORGANIC LEAVES because it grew naturally from my stash of fused scraps. I improvised the design along the way rather than planning ahead, as I do with most of my quilts. For this project, I will show you roughly what I did to create the quilt. Then I invite you to take the ideas here, play with them, have fun, and create your own organic quilt.

Materials

I made this quilt with fused scraps of my own hand-dyed fabrics. I cut the leaf backgrounds from scraps of hand-dyed lime-green and aqua-green gradations. For the leaves, I used a variety reds, oranges, and dark pinks and purples.

For some of the fillers between the blocks, I "strip pieced" fused scraps. For some of the other fillers I used miscellaneous strips of dark blues, purples, and teal for accents.

Improvising the Design Elements

1. As usual before beginning, I steam pressed my batting to take out any creases, then turned off the steam before doing any of the fusing. I placed the scraps I thought I might use, fusible side down, on a piece of release paper and lightly pressed any wrinkles and creases out of them.

2. I cut seven rectangles of various sizes from the lime-green and aqua fabrics for the block backgrounds. I created a leaf for each block by layering reds, oranges, dark pinks, and purples. Then I fused the leaves to the block backgrounds and used a rotary cutter to trim each background into an irregular shape.

3. Next I made some fused strip-sets that I planned to use as part of the filler around the leaf blocks. Fused scraps of every size went into the strip-sets (fig. 42).

42

4. With no particular plan in mind, I laid out leaf blocks on a piece of release paper, then began filling in the gaps between the blocks. I trimmed the strip-sets and filler pieces

to allow for at least a ¹⁄₁₆" overlap between adjoining elements in the design.

5. I kept arranging and rearranging pieces until I was happy with the design (fig. 43). The ORGANIC LEAVES quilt assembly diagram on page 78 shows you how the pieces went together. Figure 44 on page 78 shows you the assembled quilt.

6. Notice that I filled in two large gaps between the leaf blocks with two additional rectangles from the same lime-green fabric that I used in the blocks. I then covered them with the wavy aqua strips.

7. In the quilt assembly diagram on page 78 I've shown you some of the design elements. I started with dotted lines showing how I trimmed the elements.

43

8. As I said, this was an organic process that was more improvisational than planned. But that's the fun of it. I had a chance to play at the same time that I put all those scraps to good use.

Fusing and Finishing the Quilt

1. Once I had the quilt roughly laid out on release paper, I began lightly fusing the design elements together, continuing to adjust and trim them as the spirit moved me.

44

2. Finally, I lightly fused the design together as one unit, then fused the whole thing to a piece of batting. Though I finished my ORGANIC LEAVES quilt a little differently, you can finish your organic quilt the same way that the other quilts in this book were finished. That is, layer the fused batting on top of a piece of backing, pin the edges, then outline quilt as desired. Finally, add a hanging sleeve, binding, and a label.

ORGANIC LEAVES quilt assembly

Meet the Author

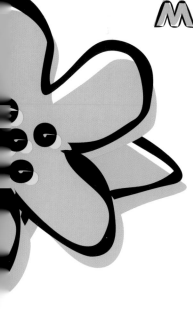

Frieda Anderson is a quilt artist, teacher, lecturer, and author. She has been making quilts for over 30 years. She has a bachelor of science degree in art history with a minor in ceramics and an associate's degree in fashion design. Frieda travels frequently to lecture and conduct workshops for quilt groups throughout the United States, and she has had articles in numerous magazines. Frieda is one of the founding members of PAQA, Professional Art Quilters Alliance, a networking group that meets in the Chicago area once a month.

Since early childhood she has been making art. She says, "My parents always encouraged me in all my artistic directions. My inspiration comes from the world around me. As an artist I try to reflect what is important in my life, my environment, and my family. Much of what I am making is the direct result of my daily walks in the woods with my dog, George."

Other AQS Books

This is only a small selection of the books available from the American Quilter's Society. AQS books are known worldwide for timely topics, clear writing, beautiful color photos, and accurate illustrations and patterns. The following books are available from your local bookseller, quilt shop, or public library.

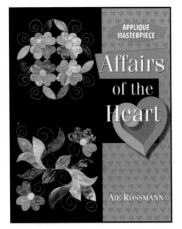

#6517   us$21.95

#6511   us$22.95

#6295   us$24.95

#6800   us$22.95

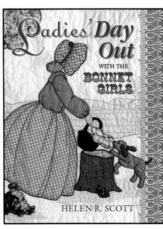

#6676   us$22.95

#6300   us$24.95

#6671   us$21.95

#6418   us$18.95

#6299   us$24.95

LOOK for these books nationally. **CALL 1-800-626-5420**
or **VISIT** our Web site at **www.AmericanQuilter.com**